BLACK BOOK OF PRICE ACTION TRADING

RITIK SHARMA

This book is dedicated to my parents

Shri Jagmohan Sharma

&

Smt Kalpana Sharma

And To my mentor, fellow traders who inspired me to pursue my passion for trading

And to those who have supported me through the ups and downs of trading and always believed in me.

May this book give you the insights and tools to succeed in the dynamic

trading world.

Contents

Acknowledgements

Writing a book is a collaborative effort, I would like to express my deepest gratitude to all the individuals who have contributed to the creation of this book on price action trading.

First and foremost, I would like to thank my family and friends for their unwavering support and encouragement throughout the writing process. Their love and support have kept me motivated and inspired, even when going was tough.

I want to thank my colleagues and fellow traders, who have generously shared their knowledge, expertise, and experiences with me over the years. Their insights and perspectives have greatly influenced the content of this book and I am grateful for their contributions. I would like to express my appreciation to the team at the publishing company who have provided invaluable guidance and support throughout the publication process. Their professionalism and attention to detail have made this book a reality.

Finally, I would like to thank the readers of this book for their interest and support. I hope that the principles and strategies outlined in this book will help you to become a more successful and profitable trader.

Thank you all for your contributions and support.

Preface

Welcome to this book on price action trading. When I first started trading, I was drawn to the simplicity and elegance of price action trading. Instead of relying on complex indicators or automated algorithms, price action trading focuses on reading and interpreting price movement in real time.

But as I delved deeper into the world of trading, I realized that price action trading was often misunderstood or misrepresented. Many traders viewed it as a "beginner's strategy" or dismissed it as too simplistic to be effective in today's markets.

I wrote this book to set the record straight. Price action trading is not only a powerful strategy but also one that can be adapted to various trading styles and timeframes. My goal is to provide a comprehensive guide to price action trading, from the basics to advanced techniques, so that traders can make informed decisions based on price movement.

This book is organized into four parts (didn't mention in index). In Part 1, I provide an introduction to price action trading and explain how it differs from other trading strategies. In Part 2, I cover the basic concepts of price action, including support and resistance, trends, and chart patterns. In Part 3, I delve into advanced price action techniques, including price rejection, hedging, and trading psychology. Finally, in Part 4, I provide practical tips for implementing price action strategies in real-world trading situations.

I wrote this book with the novice and experienced trader in mind. Whether you are new to trading or looking to expand your trading knowledge, I hope that this book will provide valuable insights and tools to improve your trading performance.

FOREWORD

As a seasoned trader with over 3 years of experience, I have seen many strategies come and go. But one approach that has stood the test of time is price action trading. In this book, the author provides a comprehensive guide to understanding and applying price action trading principles. Focusing on the most crucial factor in trading "price" allows traders to make informed decisions based on what the market is telling them.

What I appreciate most about this book is the author's clear and concise writing style in a short way with examples which makes even the most complex concepts easy to understand. The numerous charts and examples throughout the book provide a practical framework for implementing price action strategies in real-world trading situations.

But this book is more than just a technical guide to price action trading. The author also emphasizes the importance of developing a trader's mindset and managing emotions which are essential to success in trading.

What I find most compelling about this book is briefly mentions personal experience or what you found most valuable. Whether you are a novice trader or an experienced professional, this book will provide valuable insights and tools to improve your trading performance.

I highly recommend it to anyone looking to take their trading to the next level, and I congratulate the author on a job well done.

Prologue

The world of trading can be a complex and confusing place, with countless strategies and indicators vying for the attention of traders seeking an edge in the markets. But in my experience, the most successful traders are those who focus on one simple factor "Price".

Price action trading is a method of analyzing and interpreting market movements based solely on the price of an asset. By focusing on price traders can gain a deeper understanding of market sentiment and make informed decisions about when to enter or exit a trade.

But price action trading is more than just a technicalanalysis technique. It is mindset and approach to trading that requires discipline, patience, and a willingness to learn from both successes and failures.

In this book, I aim to provide a comprehensive guide to price action trading, covering the most important concepts and techniques for understanding and interpreting price movements with examples. From basic principles to advanced strategies, I will share my insights and experinces as a trader to help you develop the skills and knowledge you need to become a successful and profitable trader.

But beyond technical analysis and trading strategies, I believe that the most important factor in trading success is the ability to manage emotions and maintain a trader's mindset. Though personal anecdotes and practical advice, i will share my perspective on how to stay disciplined and focused in the face of the ups and downs of the markets.

I hope that this book will provide you with the tools and insights you need to become a more successful trader and achieve your financial goals.

Welcome to the world of Price Action Trading.

Disclaimer

About The Author

Ritik Sharma is a professional trader and educator with a unique background in the arts. Along with graduation he has also been actively trading in the financial markets, focusing on price action analysis.

He has always had a passion for finance and investing and has spent countless hours studying market trends and analyzing price movements. Their dedication and hard work had paid off, and Ritik has achieved consistent success in their trading, outperforming many seasoned professionals.

This book represents Ritik's effort to share their knowledge and experience with other traders, particularly those who are just starting out it is a comprehensive guide to price action trading, covering the most important concepts and techniques for understanding and interpreting price movements.

Despite their youth, Ritik has already achieved a tremendous amount of success and is widely recognized as an emerging talent in the world of finance. They have been invited to speak at industry conferences and featured in leading financial publications.

When Ritik is not trading or writing, they enjoy playing badminton, and gardening and are actively involved in extracurricular activities. They currently reside in Gwalior, where they are well known for their entrepreneurial spirit and their commitment to making a positive impact on their surroundings.

ABOUT THE AUTHOR

For more information, please scan this QR

I

Must know before learning Price Action

What is Trading?

Trading refers to the buying and selling of financial assets, such as stocks, bonds, commodities, currencies, and derivatives, to make a profit. Trading can be conducted by individuals or institutions and can be done through various channels, including traditional stock exchanges, online trading platforms, and over-the-counter markets.

The basic principle of trading is to buy low and sell high. Traders analyze various market factors, such as supply and demand, economic indicators, news events, and technical charts, to identify opportunities for buying or selling assets at favorable prices. They then execute trades based on their analysis, to profit from the difference between the buying and selling prices. There are various trading strategies and techniques that traders use to maximize their profits and manage their risks. Some common strategies include day trading, swing trading, position trading, and scalping.

Trading can be a lucrative and exciting activity, but it also involves significant risks. Market conditions can be unpredictable, and traders must be prepared to handle losses as well as gains. Successful traders are typically disciplined, and analytical, and have a deep understanding of the markets they trade in.

Types of Trading?

There are several types of trading, each with its unique characteristics and objectives. Some of the most common types of trading are:

- **Day Trading**: This is a type of trading where traders buy and sell financial assets within the same trading day, to profit from short-term price movements.

- **Swing Trading**: In swing trading, traders hold positions for several days or weeks, to capture medium-term price movements.

- **Position Trading**: This is a long-term type of trading where traders hold positions for several months or even years, to profit from major trends in the markets.

- **Scalping**: Scalping is a type of trading where traders make multiple trades throughout the day, holding positions for only a few minutes or seconds, to profit from small price movements.

- **Algorithmic Trading**: Also known as automated trading or black-box trading, algorithmic trading involves using computer programs and algorithms to execute trades automatically based on pre-defined rules and parameters.

- **High-Frequency Trading**: High-frequency trading involves using computer algorithms to execute a large number of trades at very high speeds, often in milliseconds, to profit from small price movements.

- **<u>Forex Trading</u>**: Forex trading involves buying and selling currencies in the foreign exchange market, to profit from fluctuations in exchange rates.

- **<u>Options Trading</u>**: Options trading involves buying and selling options contracts, which give the buyer the right to buy or sell an underlying asset at a predetermined price within a specified time frame.

- **<u>Futures Trading</u>**: Futures trading involves buying and selling futures contracts, which represent an agreement to buy or sell an underlying asset at a predetermined price and date in the future.

Each type of trading requires different skills, strategies, and risk management techniques, and traders must choose the type of trading that best suits their goals and preferences.

What is a Trading chart?

A trading chart is a visual representation of the price and volume movements of a financial asset over time, such as a day, a week, a month, or even longer. The most common types of trading charts are line charts, bar charts, and candlestick charts. Each type of chart displays the data in a different way, but they all have the same purpose of helping traders and investors to analyze the price movements of an asset and make informed decisions.

Types of Trading Chart

There are several types of trading charts used by traders and investors to analyze market trends and make trading decisions. The most commonly used types of trading charts are explained on the next page:

Line Chart: A line chart is the simplest and most basic type of trading chart. It shows the closing prices of an asset over a period of time, connected by a straight line. Line charts are useful for showing long-term trends and are commonly used by technical analysts to identify support and resistance levels, the chart below shows what a line chart looks like :

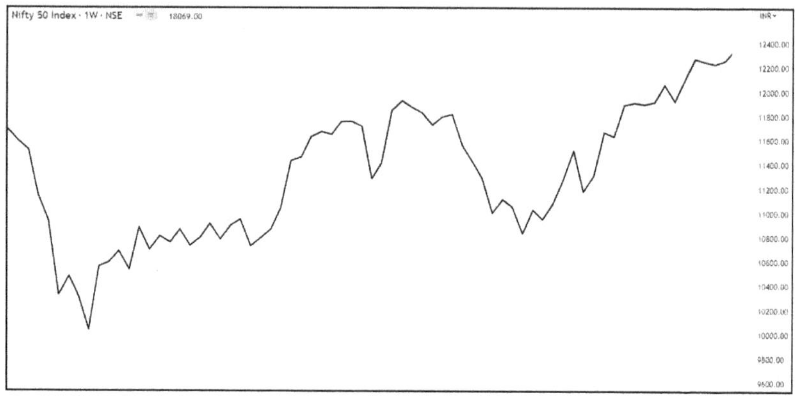

figure 1.1

Bar Chart: A bar chart shows the open, high, low, and closing prices of an asset for a given time period. Each bar represents a single period, with the height of the bar indicating the price range for that period.

Bar charts are frequently used to show comparisons between different types of data. Depending on the chart's orientation, the bars can be horizontal or vertical. Each bar's height or length represents the value of the data being presented.

Bar charts are useful for identifying price trends and patterns, and for making trading decisions based on technical analysis, *figure 1.2* shows you what a bar chart looks like :

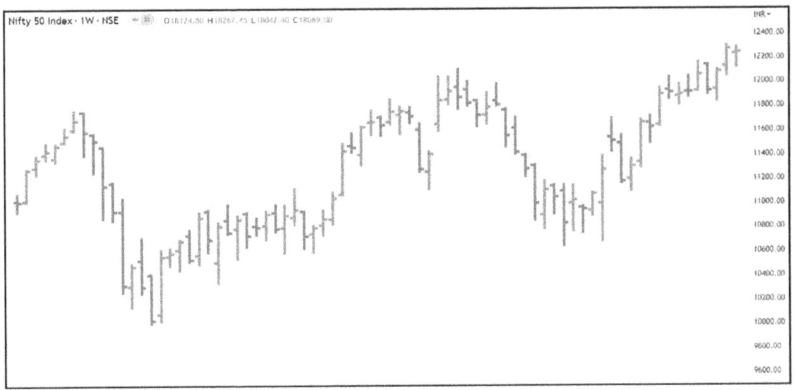

figure 1.2

Candlestick Chart: A candlestick chart is similar to a bar chart, but it provides additional information by showing the opening and closing prices as well as the price range for each period.

The body of the candlestick represents the price range between the opening and closing prices, while the wicks or shadows represent the high and low prices.

Candlestick charts are commonly used in technical analysis to identify patterns such as doji, engulfing patterns, and harami patterns.

Candlestick charts are widely used in technical analysis of financial markets, as they provide a visual representation of price movements and can help identify patterns and trends.

Traders and investors may gain perspective trading opportunities by analyzing the patterns and formations of candlesticks over time.

On the next page *figure 1.3* shows you what a candlestick chart looks like.

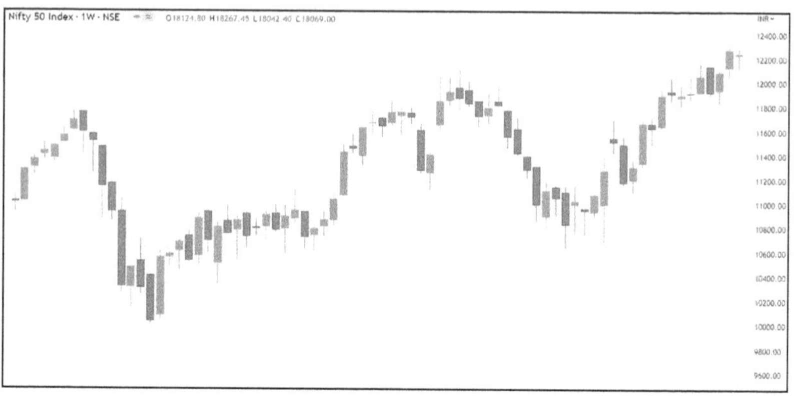

figure 1.3

<u>Point and Figure Chart</u>: A Point and Figure chart is a type of chart that uses X's and O's to represent price movements. X's represent price increases, while O's represent price decreases as shown in *figure 1.4*. Point and Figure charts are useful for identifying long-term trends and for filtering out market noise.

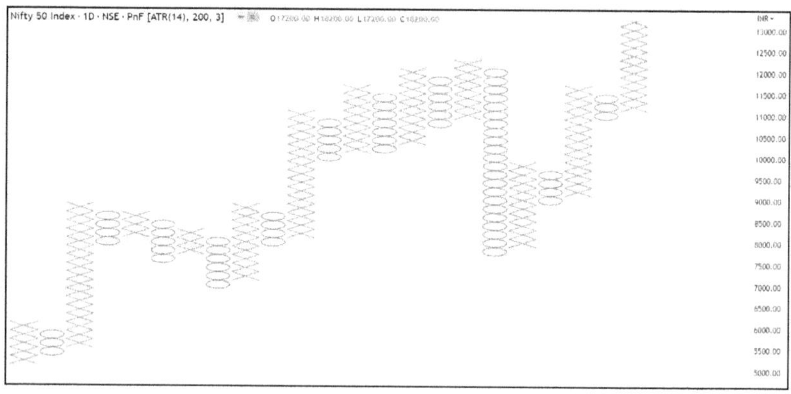

figure 1.4

Renko Chart: A Renko chart is a type of chart that uses price movements to create boxes or bricks that are either colored red or green. A green brick indicates a price increase, while a red brick indicates a price decrease. Renko charts are useful for identifying long-term trends and filtering out market noise. It looks the same as a candlestick chart but has minor differences in its patterns :

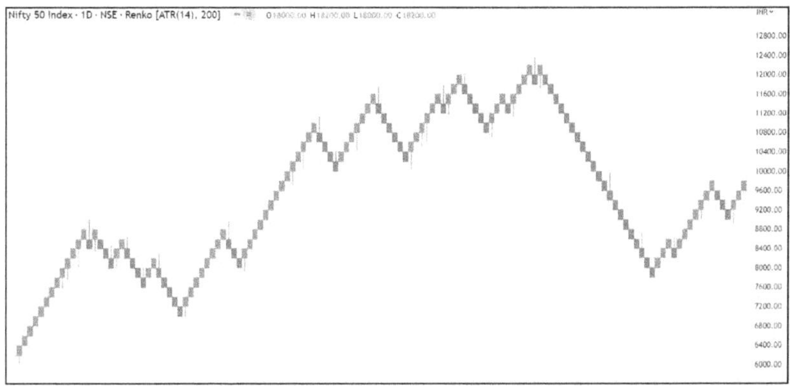

figure 1.45

Each type of trading chart has its own strengths and weaknesses, and traders may choose to use different types of charts depending on their trading style and the asset they are trading.

II

Introduction to Price Action

What is Price Action ?

Price action trading is a trading strategy that focuses on analyzing and interpreting the movement of prices on a trading chart. This strategy is based on the idea that price movements reflect all the information that is available in the market, including economic data, news events, and market sentiment.

Price action traders use technical analysis tools such as support and resistance levels, trend lines, chart patterns, and candlestick charts to identify trading opportunities. They look for patterns and signals that indicate the direction of price movement, and use these signals to make trading decisions.

One of the key principles of price action trading is the use of price levels as a means of predicting future price movements. Support and resistance levels are used to identify areas where price may bounce off or break through, and trend lines are used to identify the direction of the trend.

Price action traders also look for candlestick patterns, such as doji, engulfing patterns, and harami patterns, which can indicate a reversal or continuation of the trend. They may also use indicators such as moving averages, relative strength index (RSI), and stochastic oscillator to confirm or validate their analysis.

Price action trading requires discipline and patience, as traders must wait for clear signals and patterns to emerge before making trading decisions. It also requires a thorough understanding of technical analysis and market psychology, as traders must be able to interpret the signals and patterns in the context of market conditions and trends.

Why Price Action?

Price action trading is a popular approach to trading financial markets that involves analyzing the movement of prices on a chart to identify trading opportunities. Here are some reasons why traders might choose to use price action trading:

- **Simplicity**: Price action trading is a simple and straightforward approach to trading. Unlike other trading methods that rely on complex indicators and algorithms, price action trading focuses on reading and interpreting the natural movements of prices on a chart.
- **Flexibility**: Price action trading can be used on any financial market, including stocks, forex, commodities, and cryptocurrencies. This makes it a versatile approach that can be adapted to different market conditions and trading styles.
- **Effective risk management**: Price action trading typically involves using price levels to set stop-loss orders and profit targets, which can help traders manage risk more effectively. By setting clear risk parameters, traders can minimize their exposure to losses and maximize their potential profits.
- **Focus on market sentiment**: Price action trading is based on the idea that market sentiment is reflected in price movements.

By studying price action, traders can gain insight into the psychology of the market and use this information to make informed trading decisions.

- **Ability to trade in real-time**: Price action trading can be used in real-time trading situations, such as day trading or scalping. Traders can use price action to identify short-term trading opportunities and make quick trading decisions based on current market conditions.

Overall, price action trading can be a powerful approach to trading financial markets, offering simplicity, flexibility, effective risk management, a focus on market sentiment, and the ability to trade in real time.

Advantages

- Simplicity
- Flexibility
- Effective risk management
- Focus on market sentiment
- Real-time trading

Disadvantages

- Subjectivity
- Time-consuming
- Risk of false signals
- Lack of precision
- Limited use in certain market conditions

III
Support

What is support?

A price level at which a financial asset has historically seen buying pressure, resulting in a temporary stop or reversal of a downward market trend, is referred to be support in price action trading

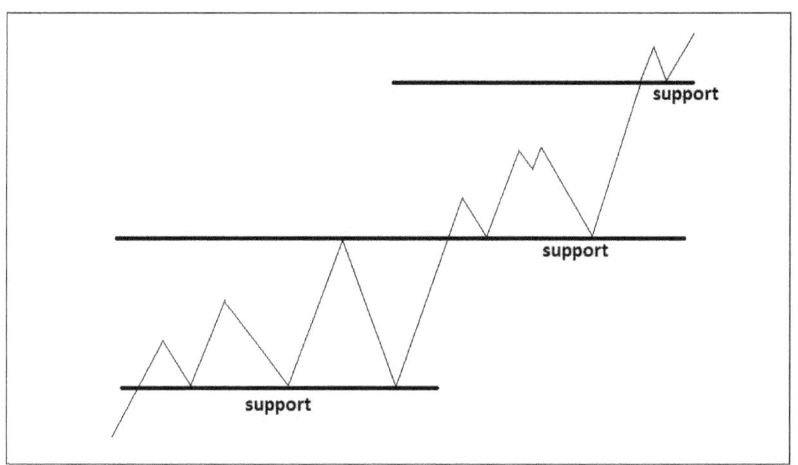

figure 3.1

In other words, support represents a level at which the price of an asset is likely to "bounce back" up after experiencing a decline, due to a higher demand for the asset at that price level. You can see figure 3.1 for a better understanding.

There are different types of support levels in price action trading, including:

- **Horizontal support:** This is a support level that is defined by a horizontal line drawn across previous lows on a price chart.
- **Dynamic support:** This refers to a support level that is defined by a moving average or trend line, which changes over time as new price data is added to the chart.
- **Psychological support:** This is a support level defined by a round number or a psychologically significant price level, such as $50 or $100.

From these three, horizontal support is the most important support for the price movement you can simply find this by analyzing the chart in the big time frame. The chart below shows all the support in the candlestick chart by this you can easily get what I am trying to say:-

figure 3.2

Traders typically use support levels in conjunction with other technical indicators and trading tools to confirm their trading decisions and manage their risk. For example, traders may use a stop-loss order placed below the support level to limit their potential losses if the price breaks below the support level and continue to decline. Overall, support is an essential concept in price action trading that can help traders identify potential trading opportunities and manage their risk.

What is a support zone?

There is only a small difference between the horizontal support line and the zone. When you are unable to find a horizontal support line because of the unstable price reversal then you can simply draw a zone (a rectangular shape area) near the price-taking reversal as shown in figure 3.3

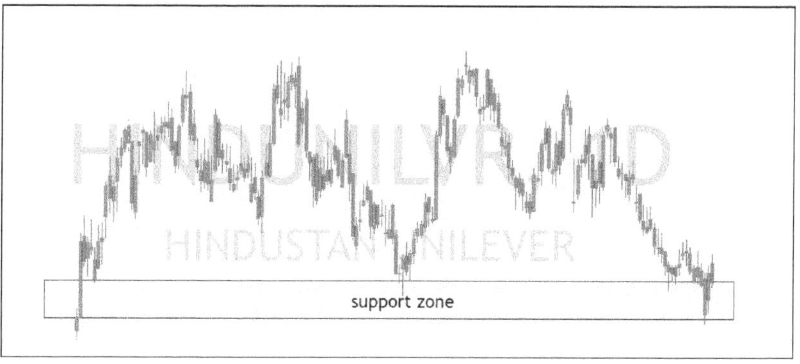

figure 3.3

Now we will see how to identify the support level in a candlestick chart on the next page.

Steps to Identify the support level

Simply follow the steps I have given below and practice, spent time with charts so you can learn to identify the right price level.

1.**<u>Select the time frame</u>**: If you want to find support for a long time then you should use a higher time frame (weakly or monthly) and for the short time you should use a small time frame (4 hours or 1 day).

I have used a 1day timeframe for short time support As shown in figure 3.4 below:-

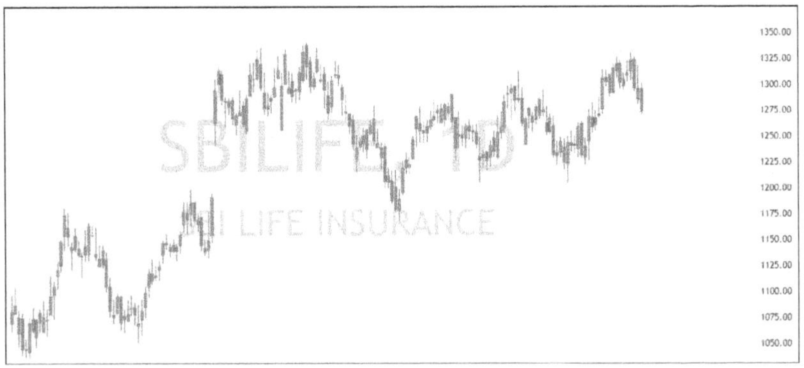

figure 3.4

2.**<u>Mark highs and lows</u>**: Identify the price level where the price has bounced back up from a previous low and mark all the points of highs and lows as shown on the next page in *figure 3.5*.

These are the levels at which buyers have previously expressed interest in purchasing the asset, resulting in a price increase

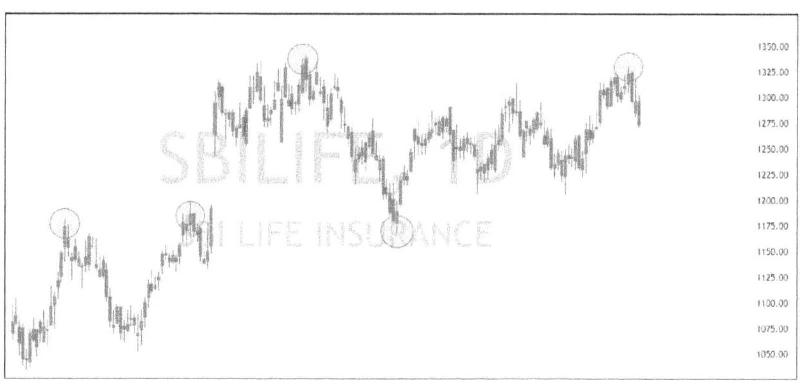

figure 3.5

3. **Connect highs and lows**: connect all the highs and lows you have marked in the previous step now you will see a horizontal line (support) was drawn by connecting those points as shown in figure.

figure 3.6

Note: The upper line act as support when the price break that level after bullish momentum.

IV
Resistance

What is Resistance?

A price level at which a financial asset has historically encountered selling pressure, resulting in a short stop or reversal of an upward price trend, is referred to as resistance in price action trading.

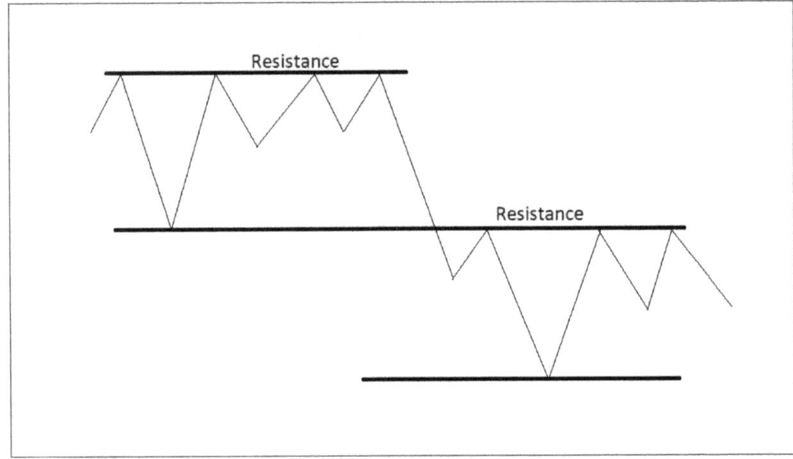

figure 4.1

In other words, it's a price level at which an asset is likely to experience selling pressure and struggle to move higher due to higher supply as shown in the above figure.

Resistance levels are often identified by looking at previous highs on a price chart and noting. Traders often use resistance levels to identify potential entry points for short positions (i.e., selling the asset) to benefit from the expected price decline from the resistance level. In real, a candlestick chart's resistance looks like (figure 4.2)

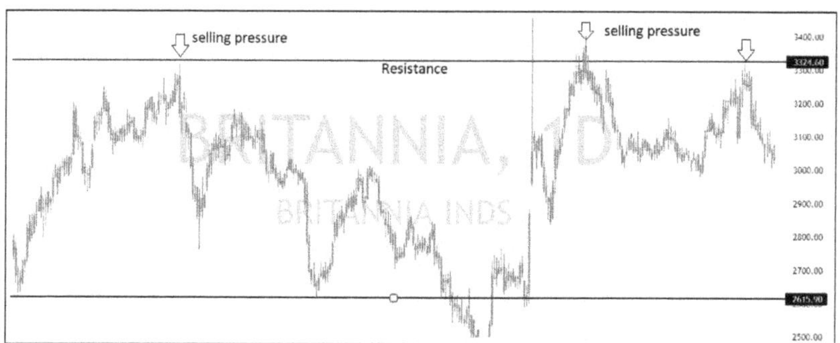

figure 4.2

There are different types of resistance levels in price action trading, including:

- **Horizontal resistance:** This is a resistance level that is defined by a horizontal line drawn across previous highs on a price chart.
- **Dynamic resistance:** This refers to a resistance level that is defined by a moving average or trend line, which changes over time as new price data is added to the chart.
- **Psychological resistance:** This is a resistance level defined by a round number or a psychologically significant price level, such as $50 or $100.

Resistance and support do almost the same thing to push the price back. Similar to horizontal support, horizontal resistance is more important for price movement. You can simply understand all three resistance in figure 4.3

figure 4.3

Traders typically use resistance levels in conjunction with other technical indicators and trading tools to confirm their trading decisions and manage their risk. For example, traders may use a stop-loss order placed above the resistance level to limit their potential losses if the price breaks above the resistance level and continue to rise. Overall, resistance is an essential concept in price action trading that can help traders identify potential trading opportunities and manage their risk.

Steps to identify the resistance level

1. Select the time frame: As I already told you in the previous chapter first you have to select the time frame according to your need that you want resistance for the long term or short term if you want to draw for the long term use big time (4 days or weakly), and for short term, you can use 1 hour to 4-hour time frame. I am selecting single day time frame as shown in figure 4.4 below:-

figure 4.4

2. Mark all swing highs: Identify the price level where the price has resisted back due to selling pressure and mark all the points as shown in figure 4.5:-

figure 4.5

3. Connect all points: connect all the highs which you have marked in the previous step now you will see a horizontal line was drawn by connecting those points as shown in figure 4.6. Ensure that the line is touching or close to the highs of the candlesticks that formed the resistance level. Be sure that you have marked the correct points if not then try to identify them by practicing more and more.

figure 4.6

Note: The lower line served as resistance for the previous price resistance and as support for the new trend.

V
Trendline

Before you can understand trendlines, you must first understand higher highs, higher lows, lower highs, and lower lows.

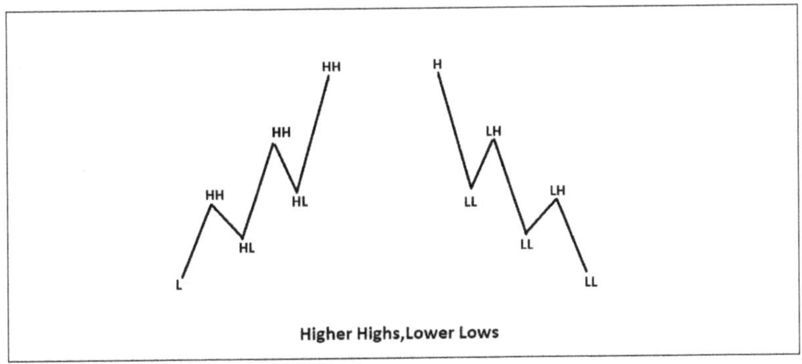

figure 5.1

Higher highs refer to the highest point reached by an asset in an uptrend.

Higher lows refer to the lowest point reached that is still higher than the previous low.

Lower highs refer to a pattern in which the high of an asset's price is successively lower than the previous high.

Lower lows refer to a pattern in which the low of the asset's price is successively lower than the previous low, indicating a downtrend.

What is Trendline?

A trendline is a technical analysis tool used in price action trading to detect and depict the direction of a trend in the price of a financial asset. A straight line drawn on a price chart connects two or more price points and is used to indicate the general direction of price movement.

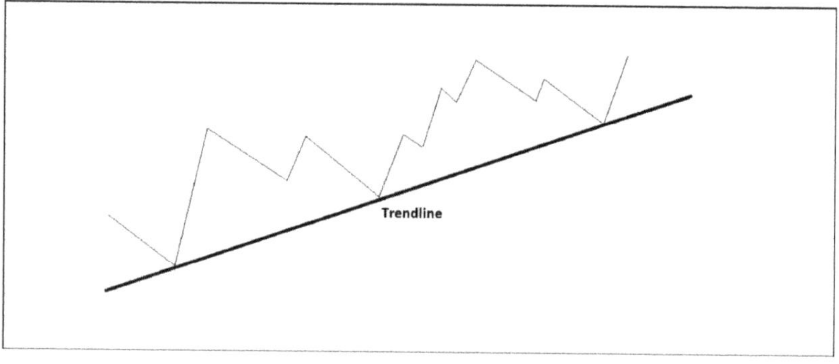

figure 5.2

There are two types of trendlines in price action trading:

- **Uptrend Trendline**: This trendline connects two or more ascending low price points on a price chart. It indicates that the price is in an uptrend, meaning that the price is generally moving higher.
- **Downtrend Trendline**: This trendline connects two or more declining high price points on a price chart. It implies that the price is in a downtrend, which means that it is generally falling.

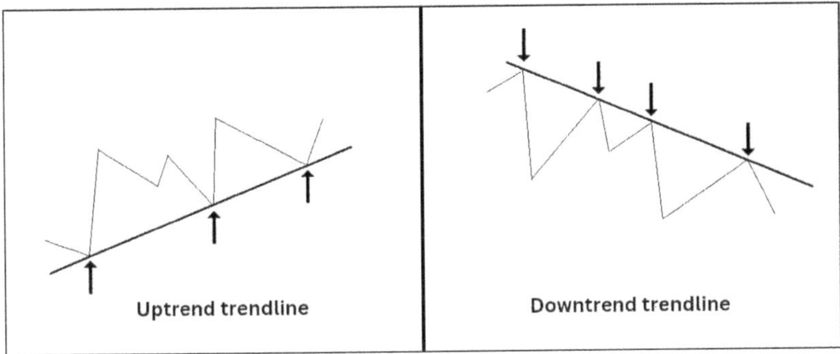

figure 5.3

Trendlines are used by traders to indicate potential entry and exit points for trades based on the trend's direction. For example, if a trader notices an upward trendline, he or she may consider purchasing the asset when the price returns to the trendline, as this may present a buying opportunity in the context of an uptrend. If, on the other hand, a trader notices a downward trendline, he or she may consider selling the asset when the price returns to the trendline, since this may present a selling opportunity in the context of a downtrend.

Trendlines can also be used to validate trade decisions and control risk in conjunction with other technical analysis tools such as support and resistance levels. Overall, trendlines are a useful tool in price action trading for identifying prospective trading opportunities and managing risk.

Steps to draw a trendline

1. Select timeframe: Choose a suitable time frame based on your requirements same as support and resistance. If you need it for a long time, choose a day or a week time frame as I choosed in figure 5.4, and for a shorter time, choose an hour or four hours time frame.

figure 5.4

2. Identify the points: As indicated in *Figure 5.5*, try to find the points where the price is bouncing back (Higher Lows).

figure 5.5

3. **Connect the points:** now simply join those points now you will see the trend line going in the upward direction with the price movement as shown in *figure 5.6*

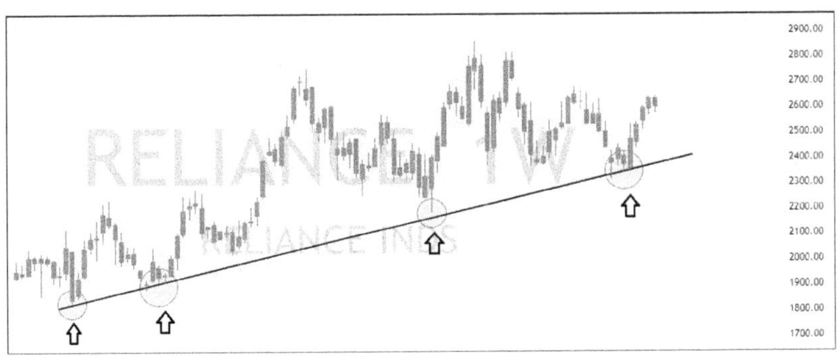

figure 5.6

VI
Market Phases

Phases of market

The market goes through multiple phases or cycles over time, which are classified into different market conditions and behaviors. While there are various ways to categorize market phases, the following are the most common:

- **Accumulation phase**
- **Markup phase**
- **Distribution phase**
- **Markdown phase**

Knowing the various stages of the stock market can allow investors to obtain insight into the market's current state and where it may be heading. Recognizing market stages allows investors to change their trading strategy and make informed decisions depending on market movements. Understanding the various stages of the market cycle can assist investors in determining the optimum moment to enter or quit the market. Investors can maximize their earnings and limit their losses by buying low during the accumulation phase and selling high during the markup period.

Investors should assess their risk tolerance and change their investment plans accordingly. For example, when the market matures and risks increase, investors may choose to minimize their exposure to the market or adopt a more defensive approach. It can also help investors in diversifying their portfolios by investing in several sectors or asset classes that may perform well in various market scenarios. This can aid in risk management and overall portfolio performance. You can clearly see all the phases of the market in *figure 6.1*. After this, we will discuss all phases one by one.

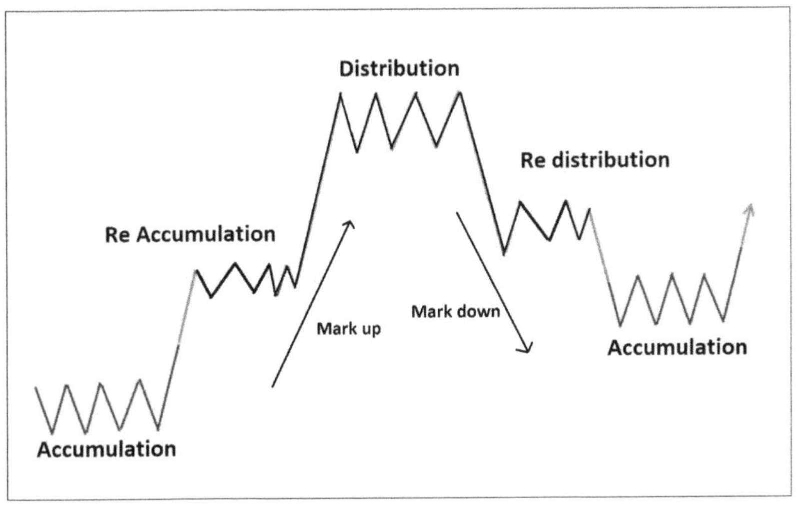

figure 6.1

Accumulation phase

This is the beginning of a market cycle, where prices are generally low and bullish traders begin to acquire and accumulate the asset. At this phase, the market may experience lower trading volumes and volatility, and prices may begin to stabilize.

Large institutional investors, such as hedge funds, investment banks, and skilled traders, start buying equities at this point. During this stage, stock prices are low, and trading volumes are also low. During this period, smart money investors are gently buying stocks in order to avoid driving up prices, as they seek to increase their position without having a large price influence.

The graph of the accumulation phase can be seen in *figure 6.2*

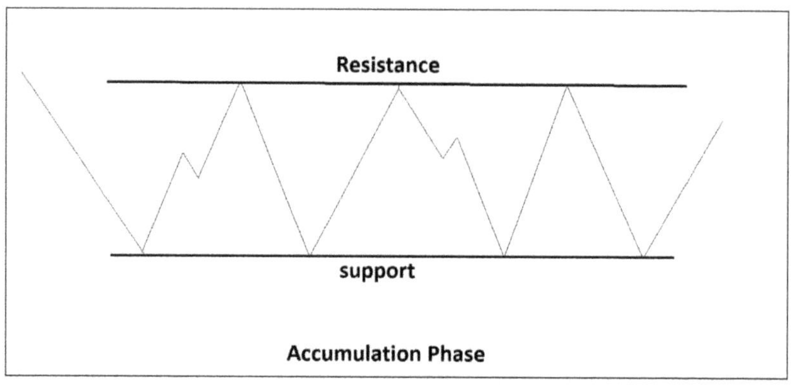

figure 6.2

The accumulation phase is distinguished by a lack of public interest in the equities, with institutional investors, who have access to inside information and research, accounting for the vast majority of investors. These investors understand that current market prices may not accurately reflect the underlying value of the stocks, but they are confident in their analysis and judgment. To uncover inexpensive companies, smart money investors conduct a review of the company's financial statements, management, and industry forecast at this stage. They seek stocks with excellent fundamentals, such as a good balance sheet, increasing revenue, and a competitive advantage in their respective markets.

Figure 6.3 shows the accumulation phase of the CNX finance chart on 1 weak time duration. Here you can clearly see that there is no volume and the price is stable in a particular price range.

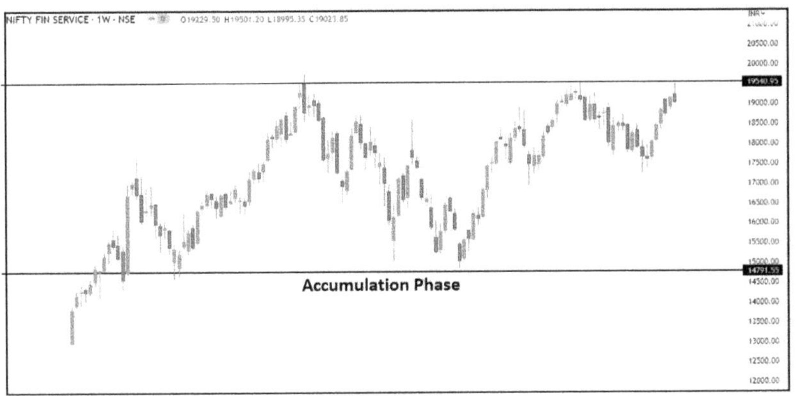

Figure 6.3

The accumulation phase is often characterized by limited market activity and price change. It is an essential stage of the market cycle because it lays the groundwork for the next stage, the markup phase, in which the smart money begins to buy more aggressively, driving up stock prices. In their respective markets, the accumulation period is a vital time for smart money investors to take a position in a stock at a favorable price since they expect the stock to appreciate in value over time.

Mark-up phase

This is the second stage of a market cycle, in which prices begin to increase as demand for the asset grows. At this stage, trading volumes and volatility may begin to climb, and smart money investors who accumulated equities during the previous stage may begin to boost their buying activities, driving stock prices higher. Trading volumes rise considerably, and retail investors become aware of the pattern and enter the market. *Here Figure 6.4* on the next page shows you the markup phase graph

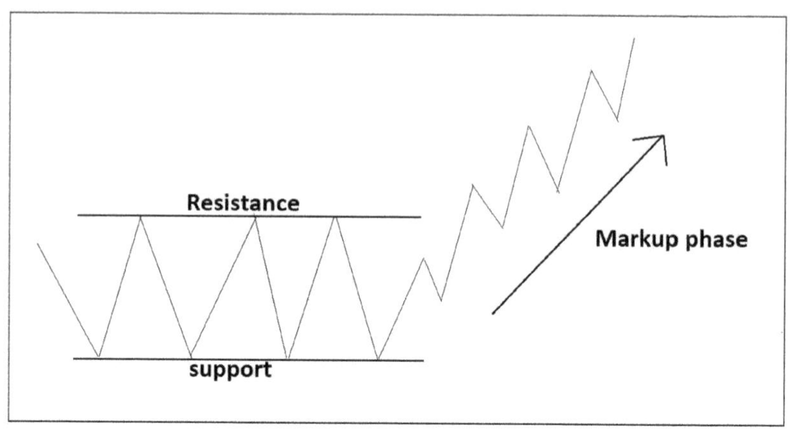

figure 6.4

Here in *figure 6.5*, you can see the candlestick chart of CNX Infra, where it is clearly seen that the investors started putting their money in the market and that's why the price and volatility in the market increased.

figure 6.5

The market exhibits a bullish tendency during the markup phase, with prices often growing gradually over time. During the accumulation phase, savvy money investors discovered basic elements such as expanding revenue, a healthy balance sheet, and a competitive edge, which lead to higher demand and price appreciation.

As the markup phase proceeds, the bullish trend may become self-reinforcing, with rising demand driving up prices, and attracting more purchasers. At this stage, market sentiment is generally positive, and investors may become more enthusiastic about the market's and economy's future.

Smart money investors may continue to accumulate positions during the markup phase, but at a faster speed, as they aim to capitalize on the rising trend. Retail investors may also enter the market at this stage, contributing to the demand and price appreciation.

It is important to keep in mind, however, that the markup phase does not persist indefinitely, and the market will eventually hit its top and enter the distribution phase, in which smart money investors begin to sell their shares to regular investors. As a result, investors must have a well-thought-out investment strategy and avoid making rash decisions based on short-term market swings.

Distribution phase

Following the accumulation and markup periods, the distribution phase is the third stage of the stock market cycle. During this stage, the market's sentiment shifts from bullish to bearish. The distribution phase is characterized by rising volatility and a gradual decrease in prices as smart money investors who purchased stocks during the accumulation phase begin to sell their holdings to less clever investors who are jumping on the bandwagon. As seen in *figure 6.6 on the next page*

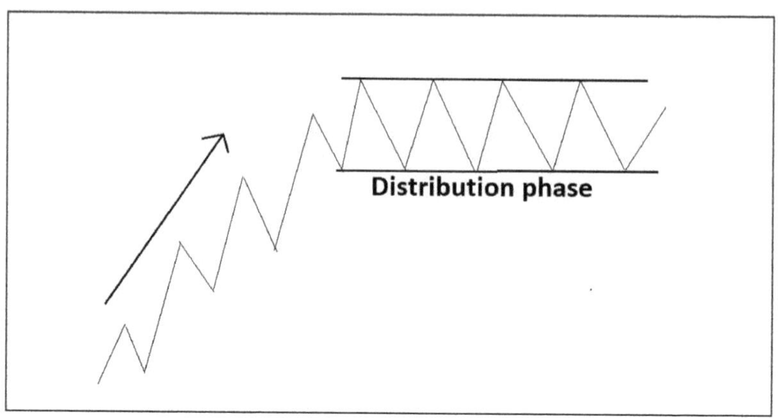

figure 6.6

In *figure 6.7* you can see the distribution phase of CNX Infra on one weak time frame here you can see that the volatility in the market increased and the price is falling because the investors now started selling the there holdings.

figure 6.7

During the distribution phase, the balance of power shifts from buyers to sellers. Stock demand begins to dwindle as smart money investors who purchased stocks during the accumulation period begin to extract profits by selling their positions to less educated investors who remain bullish on the market. This generates a supply-demand mismatch, causing prices to fall steadily. Market sentiment is typically mixed during this phase. Some investors are optimistic that the market will continue to climb, while others are growing more cautious and taking profits. As the distribution phase develops, the number of sellers increases, resulting in more volatility and price pressure.

Thus, that is a hint that the market is nearing its top, and investors should be wary about investing at this time. Investors who can spot the symptoms of the distribution phase and respond accordingly may be able to avoid losses and keep their capital.

Mark-down phase

This is the final stage of a market cycle when supply exceeds demand for the asset and prices begin to decrease as shown in *figure 6.8* Trade volumes and volatility may remain high during this period.

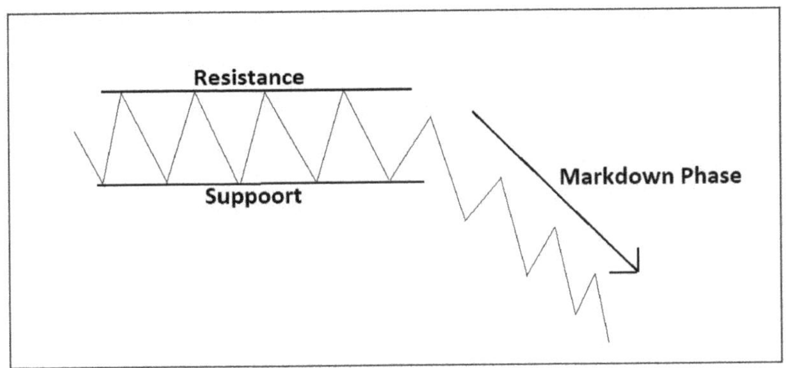

figure 6.8

During this period, the market experiences a dramatic drop in prices due to a lack of demand and an excess of supply.

Now you can see *figure 6.9 below* which shows the candlestick chart of CNX Infra on 1 weak time frame, you can see that after the distribution phase that volatility is high, and the price drops due to lack of demand and excess of supply.

figure 6.9

A combination of factors, such as an economic recession, political instability, or a major event that has a negative impact on the market, usually triggers the markdown phase. Once prices begin to fall, more and more investors panic and sell their stocks, causing prices to fall even lower. This produces a vicious cycle of selling and more falls, perhaps leading to a market crash.

Investors who did not sell their equities during the distribution phase may suffer huge losses during the markdown phase. Some investors, however, may consider this time as an opportunity to buy inexpensive firms with good long-term growth prospects.

It is important to remember that the markdown period might extend for a long time, and the market may take several years to recover. Investors who can be patient and focused on their long-term goals may be able to weather the storm and benefit from a market recovery.

Therefore, the markdown period might be unpleasant and stressful for investors, but it is also a normal part of the market cycle. Investors may better navigate the markdown period and potentially come out ahead in the long run if they are aware of the symptoms of a potential downturn and have a sound investment strategy in place.

It's important to realize that these phases aren't always well-defined or linear, and markets might go through multiple cycles in a short period of time. Furthermore, different assets and markets may experience different phases at different times, so traders must monitor market conditions and change their trading strategies accordingly.

VII
Candelstick

What is Candlestick?

A candlestick comprises four main components: open, close, high, and low. The body of the candlestick represents the opening and closing prices, while the wicks or shadows represent the highs and lows of the trading session as shown in *figure 8.1*

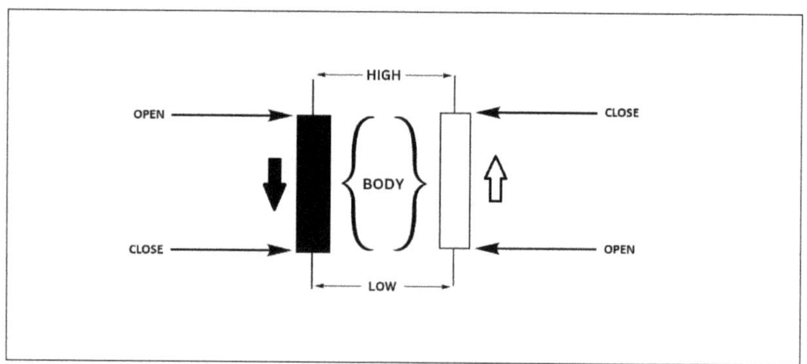

figure 8.1

Types of candlestick

There are two types of candlesticks

1. **Bullish candlestick**
2. **Bearish candlestick**

Bullish candlestick: It is a type of candlestick pattern that signals an asset's price is rising. In other words, it indicates that buyers are in command of the market and that prices are expected to rise further.

A bullish candlestick is of green or white colour. It has a long body that shows the price difference between the opening and closing values. Although certain charting software may utilize other colors, the body is commonly green or white. As *figure 8.2* shows below

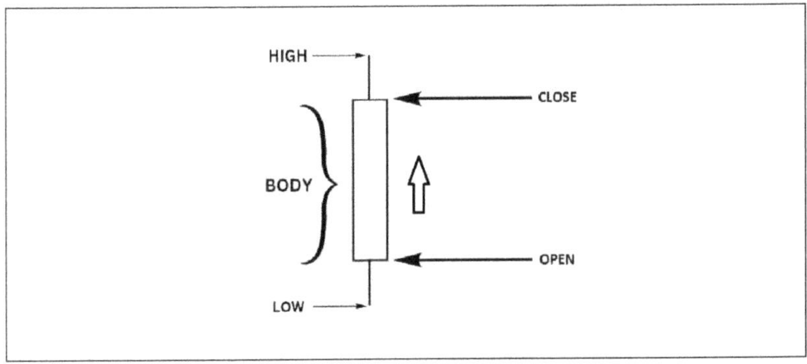

figure 8.2

When the initial price is lower than the closing price and the price climbs higher throughout the trading session, a bullish candlestick is formed. The upper shadow (or wick) is usually short in comparison to the length of the body, but the lower shadow may be greater or nonexistent.

Bullish candlesticks are frequently used by traders to detect prospective trading opportunities. For example, if a bullish candlestick appears after a period of consolidation or a decline, it may indicate that the price will likely rise further. Traders may utilize this knowledge to enter a long position in the market in order to profit from the price trend upward.

Bullish candlesticks are only one technique used by traders to assess the market. When making trading decisions, other aspects such as technical indicators, fundamental analysis, and market mood should be considered.

Bearish Candlestick: It is a type of candlestick pattern that implies a price decline in an asset. In other words, it signals that sellers have control of the market and that prices will continue to decrease.

A bearish candlestick is of Red or Black colour. It has a long body that shows the price difference between the opening and closing values. Although certain charting software may utilize other colors, the body is commonly red or black. As shown in *figure 8.3*

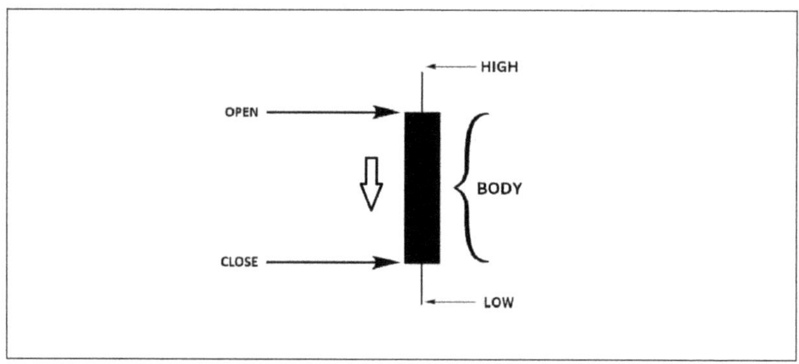

figure 8.3

When the opening price is higher than the closing price and the price moves lower throughout the trading session, a bearish candlestick is generated. The bottom shadow (or wick) is usually shorter than the length of the body, whereas the top shadow may be greater or nonexistent.

Bearish candlesticks are frequently used by traders to detect potential trading opportunities. For example, a bearish candlestick forming following a period of consolidation or an uptrend may indicate that the price is likely to decline further. Traders may utilize this knowledge to enter a market short position in order to profit from the downward price trend.

Bearish candlesticks, on the other hand, are merely one tool that traders employ to assess the market. When making trading decisions, other aspects such as technical indicators, fundamental analysis, and market mood should be considered.

Uses of Candlestick

- **Identification of price patterns:** Candlesticks can assist traders in identifying price patterns such as trends, reversals, and consolidations. This information can assist traders in forecasting future price changes and making better trading decisions.
- **Price movement visualization:** Candlesticks provide a clear and succinct picture of an asset's price movement over a particular period. This can help traders spot patterns and trends and make more educated selections.
- **Determination of support and resistance levels:** It helps traders to identify the support and resistance levels and to identify the entry and exit points.
- **Trading signal confirmation:** Candlesticks can be used to confirm other trading signals given by technical indicators. For example, if a technical indicator gives a buy signal, the trader may seek confirmation via a bullish candlestick pattern.
- **Price momentum detection:** Candlesticks can provide insights into the momentum of price movements, which can assist traders in determining the strength of a trend.

Overall, trading with candlesticks can provide traders with useful insights into price fluctuations and market patterns. Traders can improve their trading performance by better comprehending the information supplied by candlesticks.

VIII

Candlestick Pattern

Candlestick patterns can be formed in three ways:-

1. **Single candlestick pattern**
2. **Double candlestick pattern**
3. **Triple candlestick pattern**

Single candlestick pattern

A single candlestick pattern is a candlestick pattern composed of single candlesticks. It allows traders to quickly examine price action and find potential trading opportunities.

Single candlestick patterns are classified into various varieties, each with its own set of traits and implications. These are a few examples of common single candlestick patterns:

- Marubozu (green/white)
- Morubozu (red/black)
- Long candlestick (green/white)
- Long candlestick (red/black)
- Spinning top (green/white)
- Spinning top (red/black)

- Doji
- Hammer
- Inverted hammer
- Shooting star

These candlesticks are divided into two parts as given below:

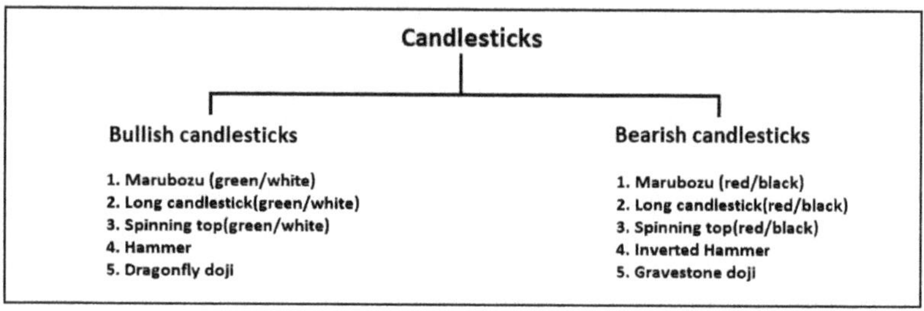

Now one by one we will discuss all the candlesticks

1. Marubozu Candlestick

A marubozu candlestick is a single candlestick pattern with a long body and no or very little shadows/wicks, as shown in *figure 9.1* on the next page. It is a Japanese phrase that means "shaved" or "close-cropped," and it refers to the candlestick having no or very little top or bottom shadow. Marubozu candle formations can be found on any time frame chart. The pattern signals it could be either a strong uptrend or a strong downtrend.

Marubozu candlesticks are frequently used by traders to detect prospective trading opportunities, such as buying a long position when a bullish marubozu appears or entering a short position when a bearish marubozu emerges. Marubozu candlesticks are only one tool that traders use to analyze the market, and they should be used in conjunction with other tools such as technical indicators and fundamental analysis.

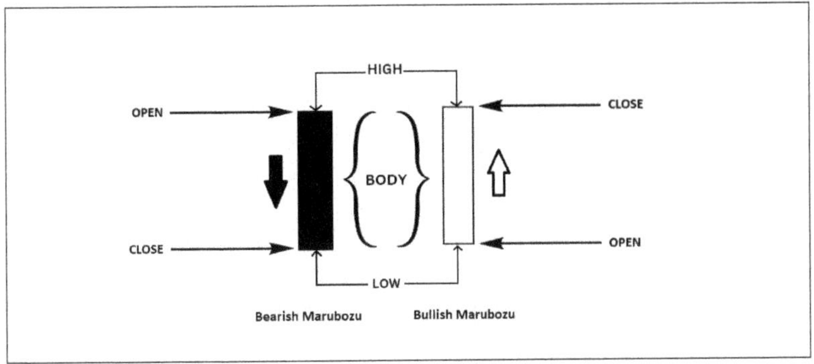

figure 9.1

Marubozu (green/white) It is also known as bullish marubozu indicates that buyers dominated the market throughout the trading session, with the price opening near the day's low and closing near the day's high. It indicates a strong bullish sentiment and indicates that the price is likely to rise further. It can be formed near support, in the middle, or near resistance as shown in *figure 9.2*

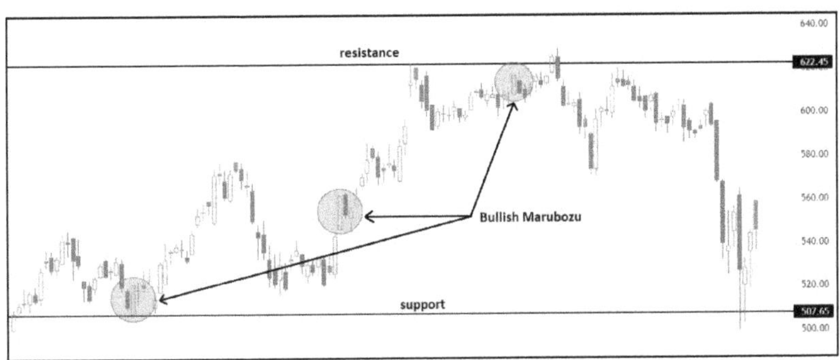

figure 9.2

Marubozu (red/black): It is also known as bearish marubozu indicates that sellers have dominated the market throughout the trading session, with the price opening at the day's high and ending near the day's low. It reflects a strong adverse mood and indicates that the price is likely to decline further. Like bullish marubozu, this can be also formed near support, in the middle, or near resistance as shown in *figure 9.3*

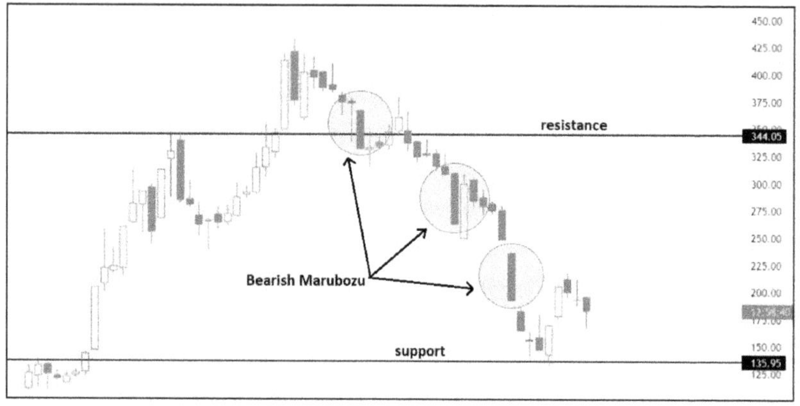

figure 9.3

2. Long candlesticks:

A long candlestick is a single candlestick pattern with a long body that represents a significant price change throughout the trading session. The difference between the opening and closing prices for the period determines the length of the body, with a long body suggesting a considerable price shift.

Long candlesticks can suggest a strong market trend and give traders useful information when assessing price movement. For example, a long bullish candlestick forming during an uptrend indicates that buyers remain in control and that the upswing is likely to continue. A long bearish candlestick forming during a downturn indicates that sellers remain in charge and that the decline is likely to continue, both candlesticks can be seen in *figure 9.4*

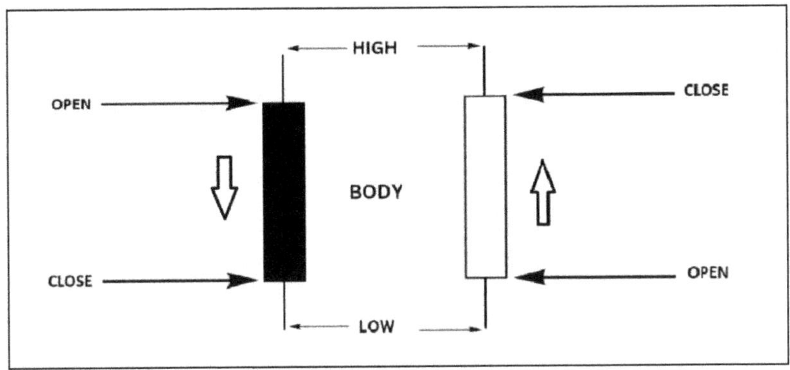

figure 9.4

It should be utilized in conjunction with other instruments like technical indicators and fundamental analysis. Traders should also be aware of potential market dangers and use appropriate risk management when trading. Long candlesticks can be bullish or bearish depending on whether the closing price is greater than or less than the initial price. Now we will talk about the bullish long candlestick below:

Long candlestick (green/white): It is also known as a bullish long candlestick, A long bullish candlestick has a long green/white body, indicating that buyers have been in control throughout the trading session and that the price has risen significantly. Longer the candlestick stronger the bullish momentum.

A long bullish candlestick can form after a period of consolidation or a downtrend, indicating a potential reversal in the price trend as shown in *figure 9.5*. I have used a chart of Eicher motors in 1-day time frame where you can see clearly that the long bullish candlestick was formed after consolidation when the trend changes to the uptrend.

figure 9.5.

Long candlestick (red/black): This candlestick also known as the long bearish candlestick, is a single candlestick pattern with a long red/black body that indicates that sellers have been in control during the trading session and that the price has dropped significantly. A considerable price movement throughout the period is represented by the length of the body, with a lengthy body suggesting a significant price shift.

When a lengthy bearish candlestick emerges, it indicates that the market has significant bearish momentum and that the price is likely to fall further. It might be seen as a signal for traders to enter a short position or exit a long position.

Long bearish candlestick can form after a period of consolidation or an uptrend, indicating a potential reversal in the price trend as shown in *figure 9.6,* I have used MRF LTD stock in a weak time frame where it can be seen that two bearish long candlesticks formed when the uptrend changes into the downtrend after touching the resistance due to selling pressure.

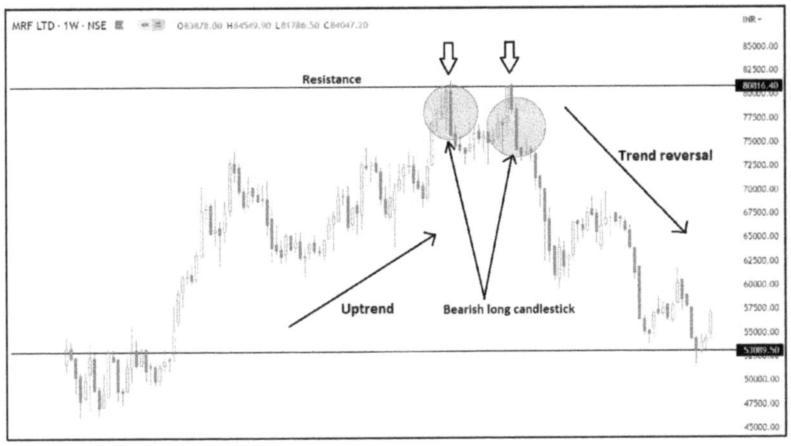

figure 9.6

3. *Spinning top:*

A spinning top candlestick is a single candlestick pattern with a small body and identical length upper and lower shadows.

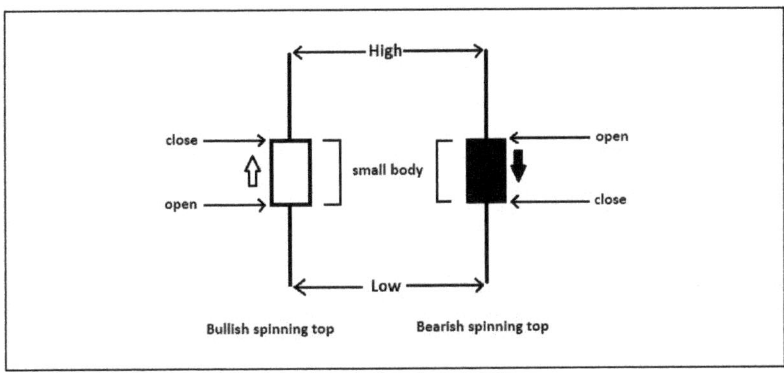

figure 9.7

As shown in *figure 9.7*, The small body shows a limited price range between the opening and closing prices, while the upper and lower shadows indicate price movement during the trading session.

A spinning top candlestick indicates market hesitation, with neither buyers nor sellers able to dominate the price action. The pattern may indicate a probable trend reversal, but it is not a strong signal in and of itself. However, before making any trading decisions, it is critical to wait for confirmation from other technical indicators or research. Which we will know about in upcoming topics.

It can occur in two cases during an uptrend, and during a downtrend:

If it occurs during an uptrend, it indicates that buyers and sellers are evenly matched and that a reversal is possible it can be seen in *figure 9.8* in that I have used Dr Reddys labs stock in 1 weak time frame you can see that during a downtrend a spinning top candlestick formed near support after that trend was reversed to the uptrend.

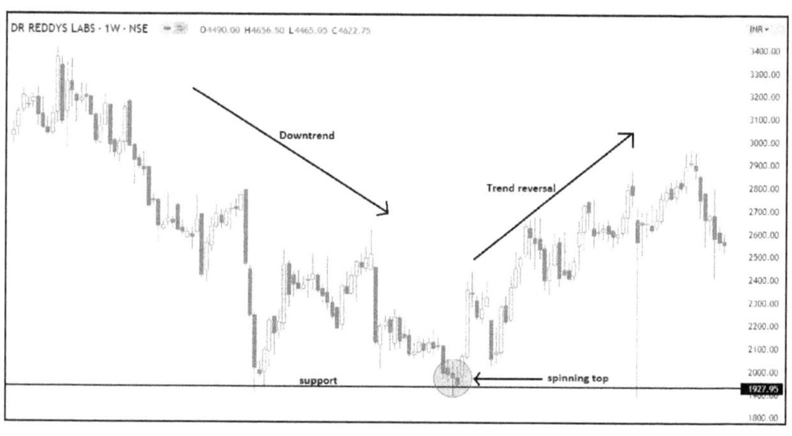

figure 9.8

On the other hand, a spinning top emerges during a decline, which indicates that sellers and buyers are evenly matched and that a reversal is possible as shown in *figure 9.9* I have used Dr Reddys stock again on 1 weak timeframe where you can see that after the formation of spinning top candlestick on resistance level, there is a decline of trend and downtrend started.

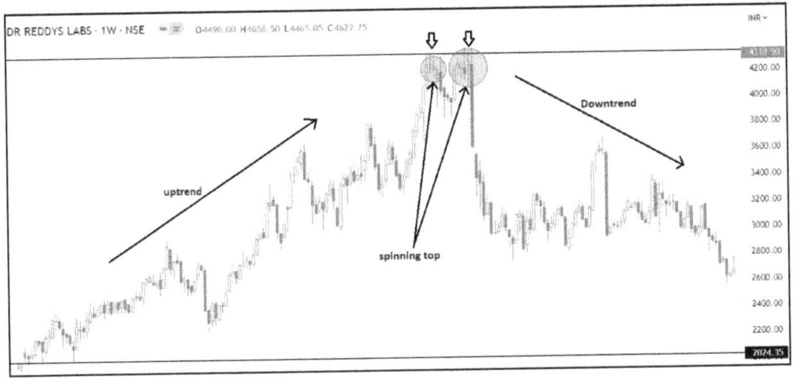

figure 9.9

4. Doji:

A Doji candlestick is a financial chart pattern that appears when an asset's starting and closing values are relatively near each other, resulting in a thin line or cross form. This pattern indicates market indecision because neither buyers nor sellers have control over the asset's price action.

The Doji pattern has several types, each with its distinct properties. some popular patterns are discussed below:-

1. Long-legged Doji:- It is a candlestick pattern that develops when a financial instrument's starting and closing prices are near to each other and the trading range (the difference between the highest and lowest prices) is quite broad. As a result, the candlestick has a long upper and lower shadow as well as a small or nonexistent true body as shown in *figure 9.10* below:-

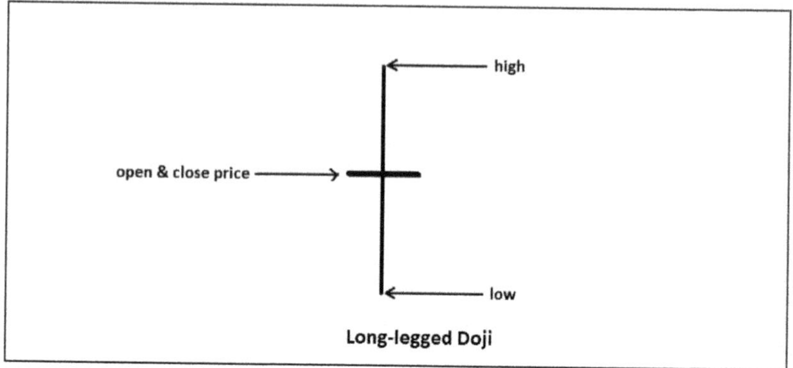

figure 9.10

The long-legged doji indicates market hesitation, as both buyers and sellers were active during the trading session but were unable to move the price significantly in either direction. *Figure 9.11* shows an example of this. I used the Indusind Bank chart to show that both sellers and buyers are active, which is why the market is consolidating and not moving in one direction, and the price is going up and down repeatedly.

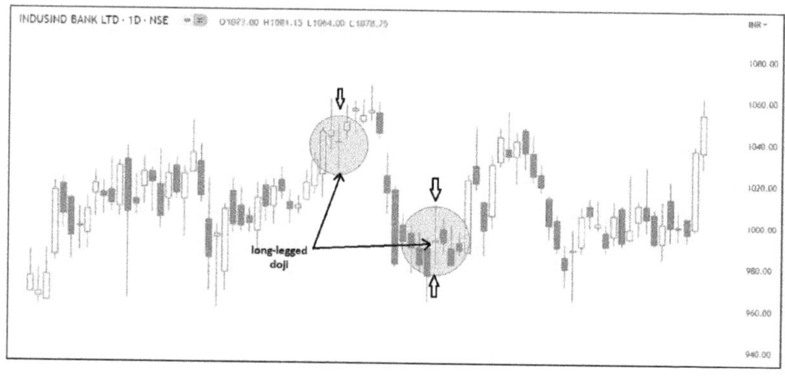

Figure 9.11

2. Gravestone Doji:- A gravestone doji is also known as tombstone doji, it is a bearish candlestick pattern that emerges on a financial chart when the opening and closing prices are the same and the day's high is equal to the opening price. The candlestick pattern resembles a tombstone with a long shadow or wick above it as shown in *figure 9.12*

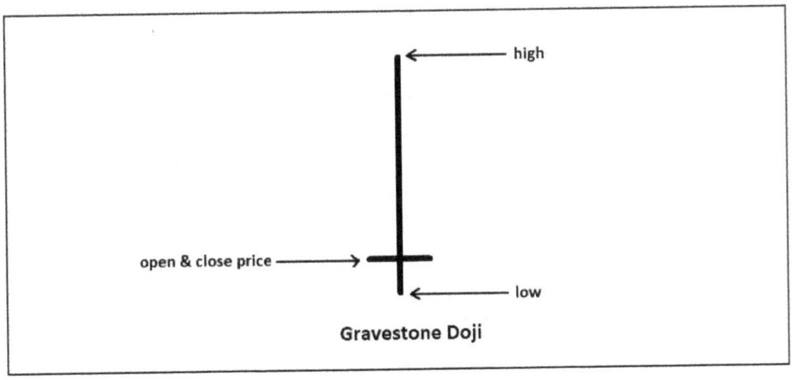

figure 9.12

The gravestone doji is a bearish reversal pattern that indicates the market is losing bullish momentum and a potential reversal is on the way. The pattern implies that buyers dominated the market at first but were unable to sustain their dominance as sellers took control, bringing prices back down toward the opening price. And its large upper shadow shows that the bulls' failed attempt to drive prices higher, while the lack of a lower shadow indicates that there is minimal purchasing support at lower levels. As a result, the bears have a stronger influence on the market than the bulls, leading to a negative bias.

In *figure 9.13* I have used Britannia Inds on a 1-day time frame chart where you can see that 2 gravestone doji candles are formed which indicates the selling pressure and sellers are pushing the price back. Some traders see this as a signal to sell or short the market.

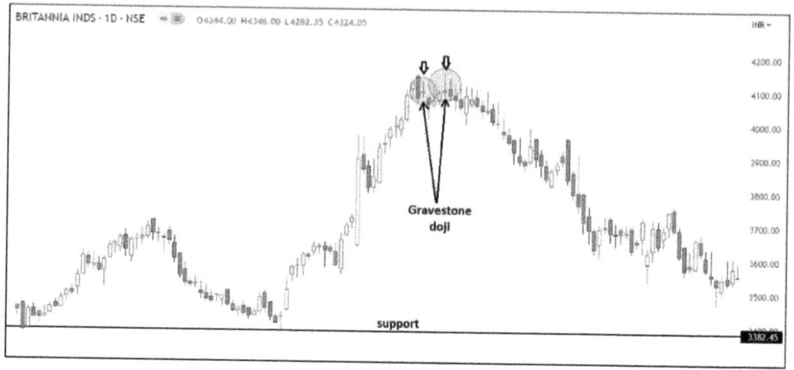

figure 9.13

3. <u>Dragonfly Doji</u>:-

The lower shadow of the Dragonfly candlestick is lengthy, there is no higher shadow, and the body is little or non-existent. as shown in *figure 9.14*. The extended lower shadow indicates that the price opened and dropped heavily throughout the trading period, but subsequently recovered and closed near the period's high.

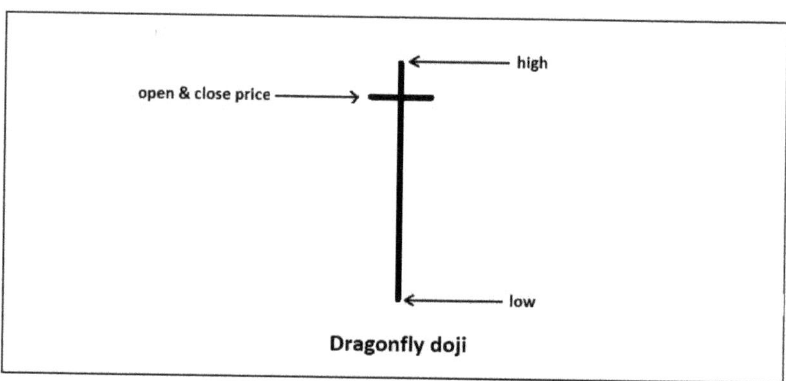

figure 9.14

When looking for prospective buying opportunities, traders frequently check for Dragonfly candlesticks. If a Dragonfly candlestick comes after a long decline, it can indicate that the selling pressure is easing and buyers are entering the market. However, before making any trading moves, traders should always check the signal with other indicators and analyses.

In *figure 9.15*, I have shown the Bajaj finance chart in 1-day time frame here, you can see that 2 dragonfly doji candles are formed due to buying pressure which indicates that buyers entered the market and moved the market in the upward direction.

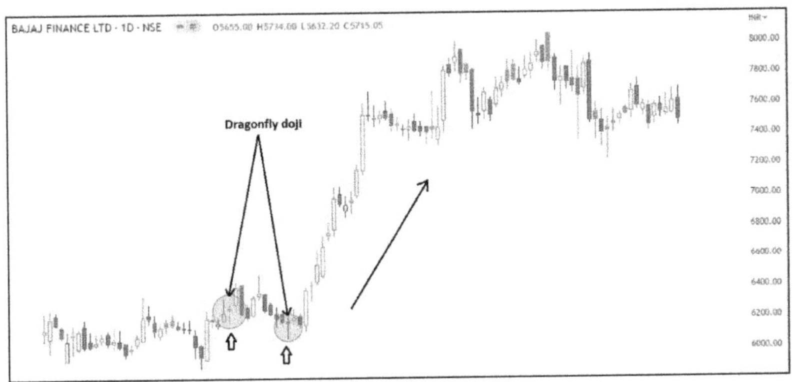

figure 9.15

5. Hammer:

A hammer candlestick is a kind of candlestick pattern in trading that might indicate a potential trend reversal. This is also known as Hanging Man candlestickThe hammer candlestick has a small true body at the top and a lengthy lower shadow that can be twice as long as the real body. The upper shadow is either very small or completely absent. It can be seen in *figure 9.16*

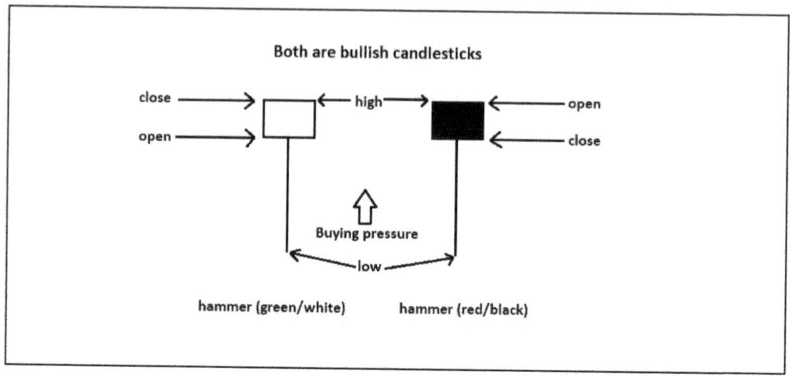

figure 9.16

The hammer candlestick can imply that sellers drove prices lower during the trading session, but buyers stepped in near the conclusion and pushed prices back up, resulting in a long lower shadow. The modest real body indicates that buyers were able to marginally raise prices but were unable to close the session above the open. The bullish hammer pattern may imply that selling pressure has been exhausted and buyers have gained control, potentially signaling a reversal of the present trend.

figure 9.17

In *figure 9.17* you can see I have used Asian paints chart on 1-day timeframe where, after consolidating a hammer candle formed near the support zone because of buying pressure and pushed the price high. The color of the candle did not affect the bullish momentum either it can be "green/white" or "red/black".

Some traders may see the bullish hammer pattern as a signal to go long, placing a purchase order or otherwise acquiring bullish positions. Others may use it as a signal to exit short positions or to place a stop-loss order to protect themselves from a possible reversal.

6. Inverted hammer:

An inverted hammer candlestick pattern is the mirror image of a standard hammer design. It is formed when the opening, high, and closing values of a candlestick are roughly the same, but with a long upper shadow and a little lower shadow, or none at all, and can indicate a probable reversal in a downtrend. You can see how an inverted hammer candlestick looks like in *figure 9.18*

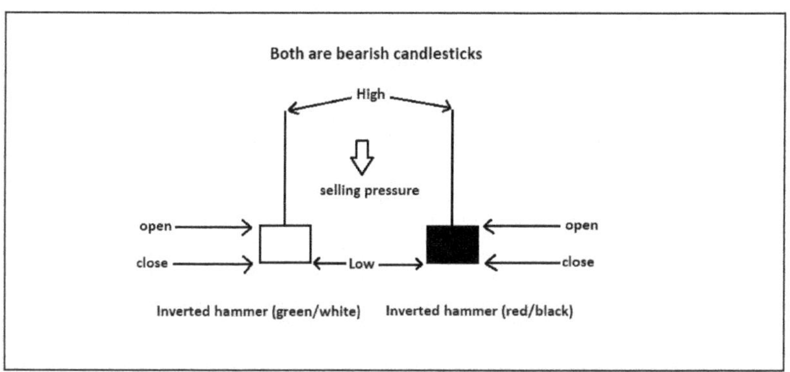

figure 9.18

The inverted hammer pattern can signal that buyers entered the market during the trading session and pushed the price higher, but were unable to maintain the momentum, resulting in a long upper shadow. The lack of a lower shadow or the absence of one implies that there was little selling pressure during the session.

Some traders may see the inverted hammer pattern as a signal to go long, place a purchase order, or otherwise acquire bullish positions. Others may use it as a signal to exit short positions or to place a stop-loss order to protect themselves from a possible reversal.

In *Figure 9.19*, you can see how an inverted hammer formed on the chart. I used a Larsen & Toubro chart on a one-day timescale, and it is evident that following an uptrend, two inverted hammer candles formed at the resistance level, and the upswing reverted into a downtrend due to high selling pressure.

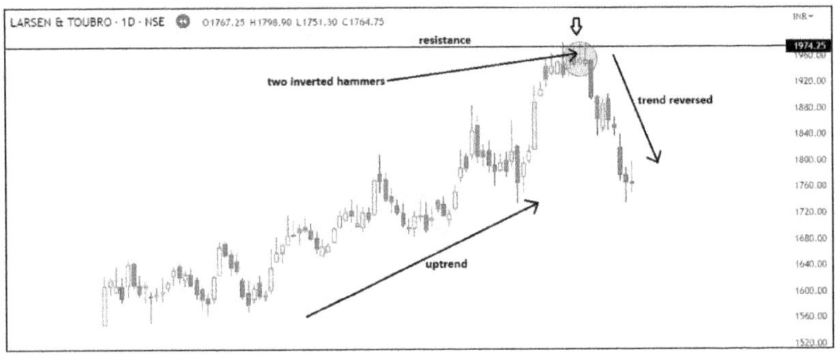

Figure 9.19

7. *Shooting star:-*

The Shooting Star candlestick has a lengthy upper shadow, a short or non-existent lower shadow, and a little body at the period's low as shown in *figure 9.20*. The extended upper shadow indicates that the price opened and rose strongly throughout the trading period, but subsequently succumbed to selling pressure and closed near the period's lows.

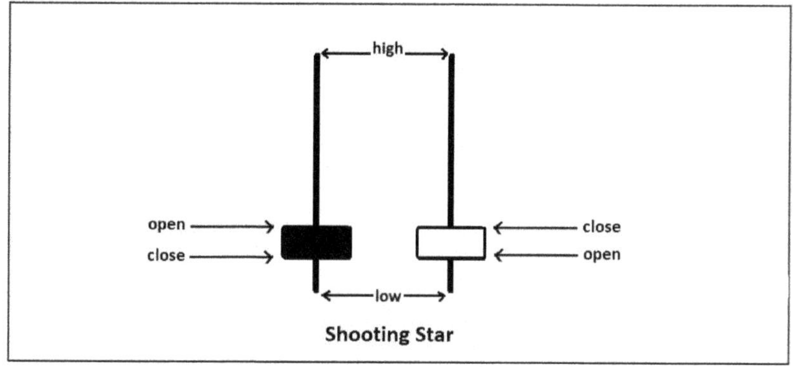

figure 9.20

When looking for prospective selling chances, traders frequently seek Shooting Star candlesticks. When a Shooting Star candlestick comes after a long uptrend, it can indicate that buying pressure is waning and sellers are entering the market.

Take a look at *figure 9.21* in which I used the Hindustan Unilever chart in 1-day time frame which clearly shows that 2 shooting star candlesticks formed due to selling pressure because sellers entered the market and due to this the price of the stock was decreasing.

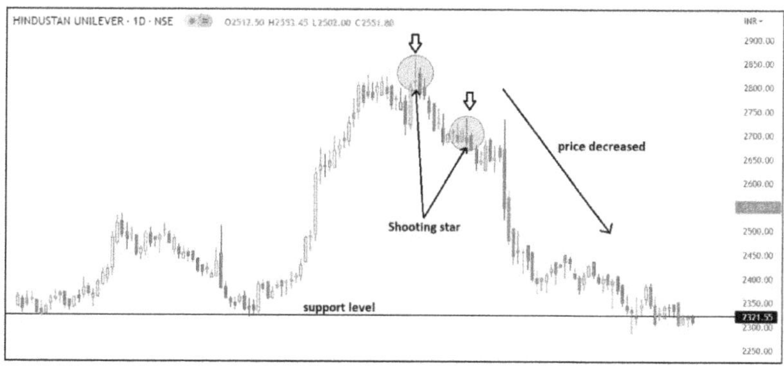

figure 9.21

<u>Note:-</u> Now that I've described why gravestone doji, inverted hammer, and shooting star are different candles, you're probably wondering what the difference is ?

These three are all doji candles and are all bearish candlesticks, but they differ slightly in their structure. For example, the body of the gravestone doji is very small, and it opens and closes at the same point, whereas the shooting star has a slightly larger body than the gravestone's, and it opens and closes at different points. On the other hand, the hammer has no wick, whereas the other two have a small wick on the downside.

Double Candlestick Patterns

The candlestick patterns which are formed by two consecutive candlesticks on a price chart are called double candlestick patterns. The pattern's first candlestick can be of any size or color, although it's usually smaller than the second. The second candlestick, on the other hand, is typically larger and oriented in the opposite direction as the first. There are various types of double candlestick patterns, each with its unique interpretation. Some of them are discussed below:-

- Bullish kicker
- Bearish kicker
- Bullish Engulfing
- Bearish engulfing
- Bullish harami
- Bearish harami
- Piercing line
- Tweezer top
- Tweezer bottom
- Dark cloud line

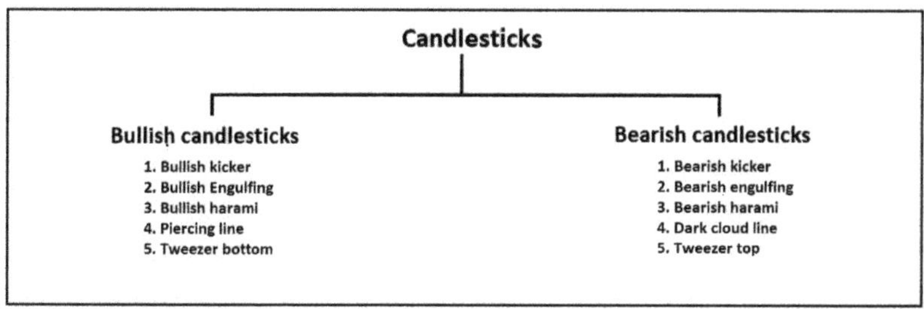

1. Bullish kicker:-

A bullish kicker candlestick pattern is a technical analysis method that traders use to spot future price reversals in financial markets. This pattern appears when the price of an asset rises suddenly and sharply, as indicated by two successive candlesticks.

In *figure 9.22,* The first candlestick in the pattern is bearish, signaling that the market is in a downtrend. The second candlestick is a bullish candlestick that starts higher than the previous day's high, indicating a dramatic shift in market sentiment and the possibility of reversing from a downtrend to an uptrend.

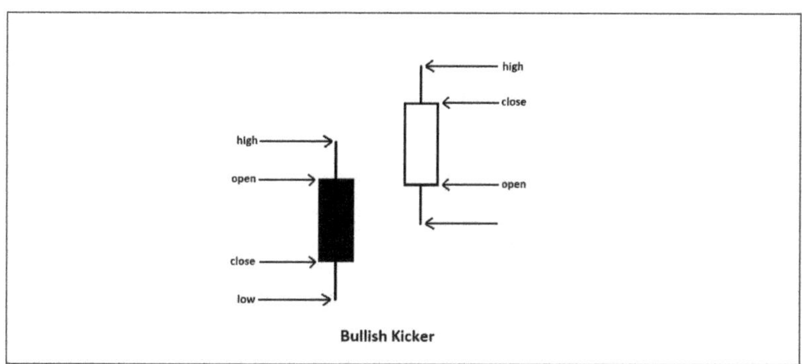

figure 9.22

This pattern is seen as a strong indication for traders to enter long positions in the market since it indicates that purchasing pressure has surpassed selling pressure and the price is expected to rise further. But, no trading system is perfect, and traders should constantly practice risk management and employ stop-loss orders to reduce their potential losses. Now I will show you how a bullish kicker works in charts, so Here I have shown you the chart of Nifty 50 chart in *figure 9.23* on 1-day timeframe here you can see clearly that Bullish kicker pattern is formed at the support zone which is bullish and the market got reverse from the support zone.

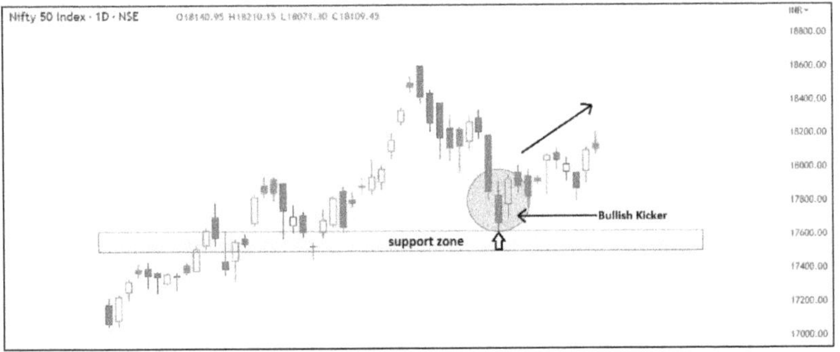

figure 9.23

2. Bearish Kicker:-

When a bullish candlestick is followed by a huge bearish candlestick that opens lower than the previous day's close, a gap is formed.

This pattern is the inverse of the bullish kicker pattern depicted in picture 9.24.

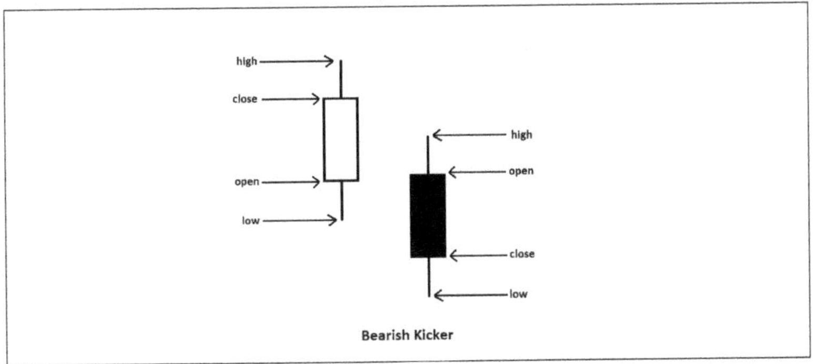

figure 9.24

It shows that formerly positive investors swiftly sold off their positions, resulting in a dramatic decrease in prices.

Traders can use the bearish kicker candlestick pattern to sell long positions or enter short positions in expectation of more market losses.

It is vital to remember, however, that the pattern should be utilized in conjunction with other technical analysis tools and methodologies in order to make sound trading decisions.

On the next page in *figure 9.25* , I have shown the "Gail India" 1-day time frame graph that indicates that when sellers enter the market near the support/resistance zone, Bearish kicker pattern forms, and instead of purchasing, traders start selling the stock, causing the price to decline.

figure 9.25

3. Bullish Engulfing:-

The bullish engulfing pattern indicates that market sentiment has shifted from bearish to positive.

It is made up of two candlesticks: a smaller bearish candlestick followed by a larger bullish candlestick that engulfs the previous bearish candlestick as shown in *figure 9.26* on the next page .

It suggests that buyers have stepped in and taken control after a period of selling pressure, pushing prices higher.

The larger bullish candlestick engulfs the previous bearish candlestick, covering its whole range, and indicating a strong bullish signal.

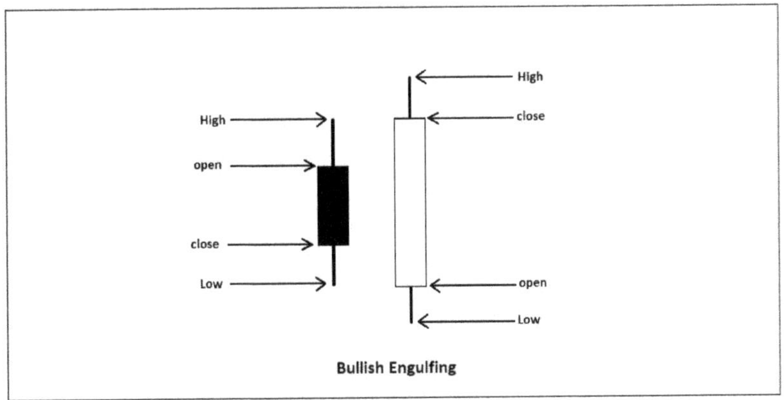

figure 9.26

This could indicate a trend reversal and the possibility of a price resurgence. However, it is not a failsafe and should be used in conjunction with other types of analysis to determine the likelihood of a reversal. In *figure 9.27*. I used a chart of the State Bank of India in a one-day timeframe, and it's clear that the bullish engulfing candlestick formed at support due to strong buying pressure, and the trend reversed from there.

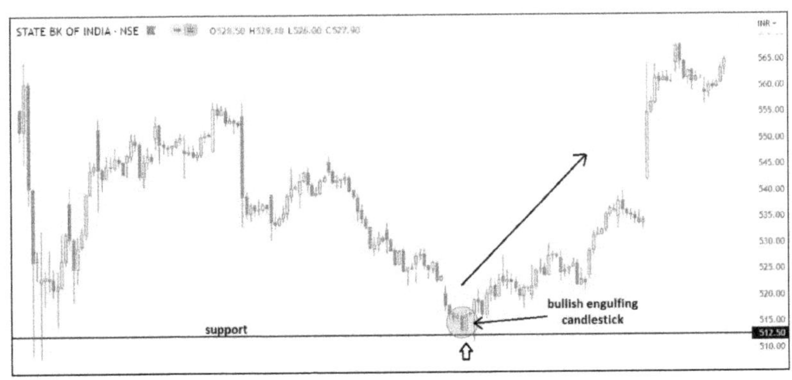

figure 9.27

4. Bearish Engulfing:-

It is made up of two candlesticks: a smaller bullish candlestick followed by a larger bearish candlestick that engulfs the previous bullish candlestick as shown in *figure 9.28*. It is a pattern that indicates a reversal of trends in the stock charts.

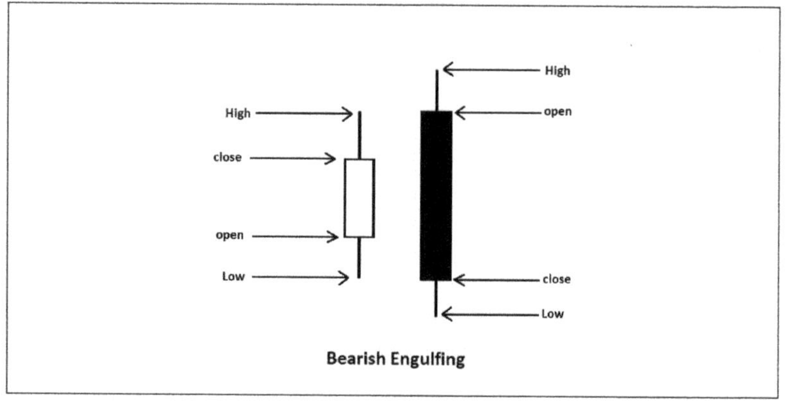

figure 9.28

It indicates that market sentiment has shifted from bullish to negative or It denotes that sellers have regained power after a period of purchasing pressure, resulting in a drop in prices. The larger bearish candlestick completely engulfs the previous bullish candlestick, suggesting a strong negative indication. When recognizing a bearish engulfing pattern, traders look for additional factors such as the overall market trend, support and resistance levels, and volume in order to validate the pattern and make informed trading decisions. Now look at *figure 9.29*, which shows a graph of Asian paint in 1-hour timeframe after a bullish trend on the support zone, and a fast reversal of the trend can be seen here bullish trend transformed into a negative trend.

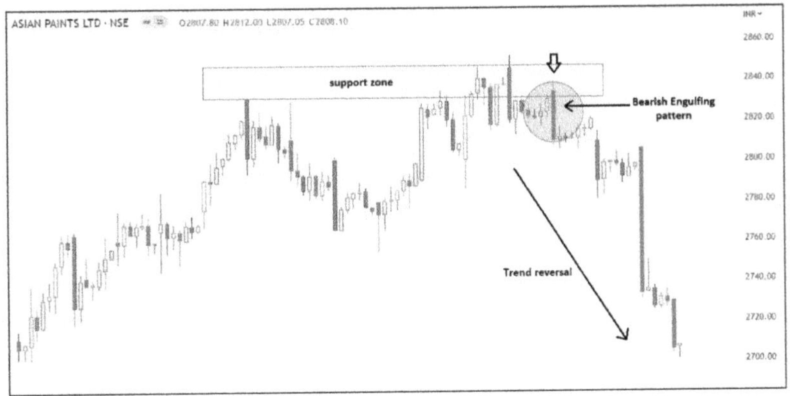

figure 9.29

5. Bullish Harami:-

The bullish harami pattern implies that market sentiment is turning positive.

It is made up of two candlesticks, the first of which is a larger bearish candlestick, followed by a smaller bullish candlestick that is completely enclosed inside the range of the preceding bearish candlestick.

It implies that, after a period of selling pressure, buyers are entering and taking control, signaling a possible trend reversal.

Figure 9.30 shows a representation of a bullish harami candlestick pattern on the next page:-

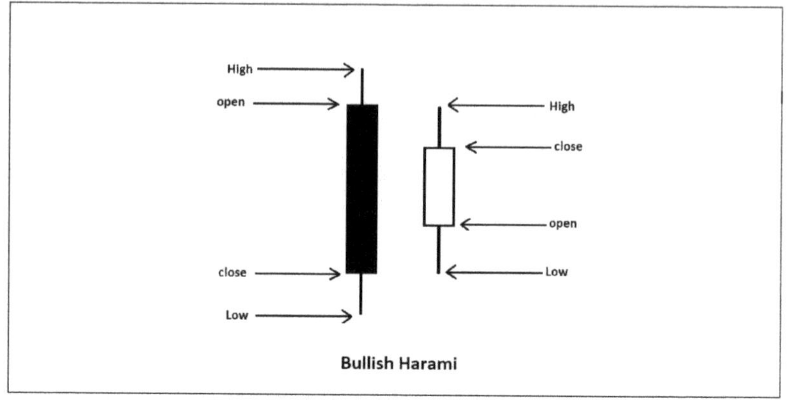

Figure 9.30

The smaller "harami" bullish candlestick is seen as a sign of market indecision, and the fact that it falls inside the range of the previous bearish candlestick is interpreted as a positive indicator.

A bullish harami pattern is commonly viewed as a potential purchasing opportunity by traders and investors, as it may indicate the possibility of a price rebound.

But, like with any technical pattern, it should be used in conjunction with other forms of analysis to validate the likely reversal.

Figure 9.31 demonstrates how this pattern can produce a market reversal, on trendline bullish harami pattern is formed owing to higher purchasing pressure and so buyers are more dominant than sellers, causing price stock to grow

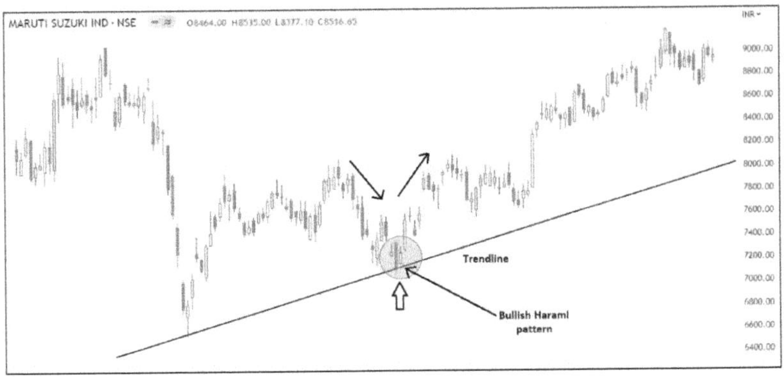

figure 9.31

6. Bearish Harami:-

The bearish harami indicates that bullish momentum is fading and the bears are taking control. Itis derived from the Japanese word for "pregnant," as the smaller bearish candle appears concealed within the larger bullish candle.

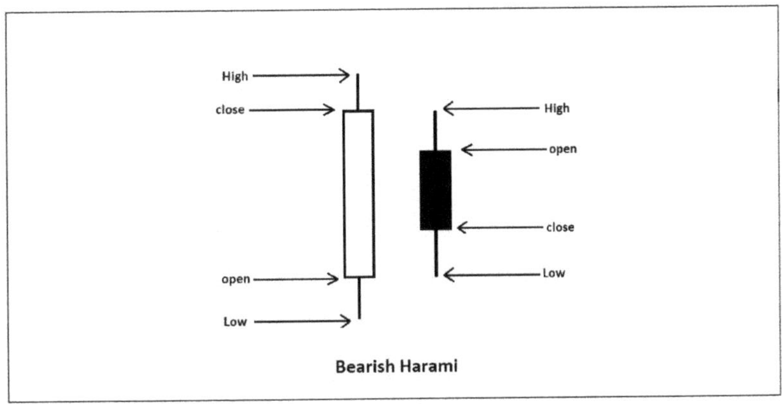

figure 9.32

During an upswing, the bearish harami candlestick pattern emerges and suggests a potential trend reversal. It is formed by two candles a massive bullish candle, followed by a smaller bearish candle that is completely contained inside the range of the preceding bullish candle as shown in *figure 9.32*. It is regarded as a warning sign for traders to exercise caution and consider taking profits or starting bearish bets. As it portrays a struggle between bulls and bears, the smaller bearish candle inside the pattern is interpreted as a sign of hesitation or a possible trend reversal. In the chart below, we can see that after the formation of a bearish pattern, the trend has completely reversed and the price has plummeted due to intense selling pressure.

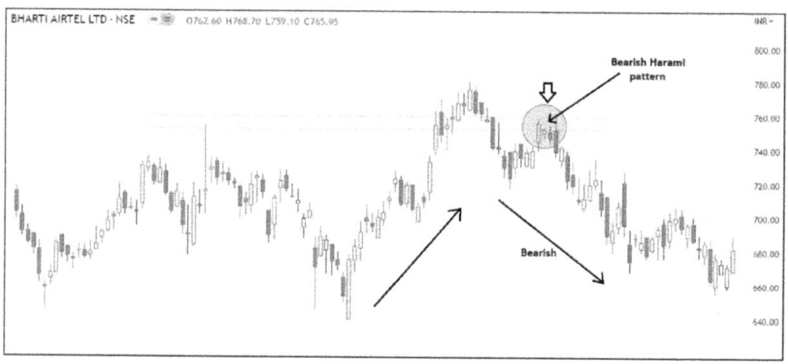

figure 9.33

7. Piercing line:-

It is a bullish reversal candlestick pattern that might offer a potential purchasing signal to traders.It usually happens towards the end of a downtrend and is made up of two candles. The first candle is a massive bearish candle, which is followed by a smaller bullish candle that "pierces" more than halfway through the previous bearish candle's body. It can be seen in *figure 9.34:-*

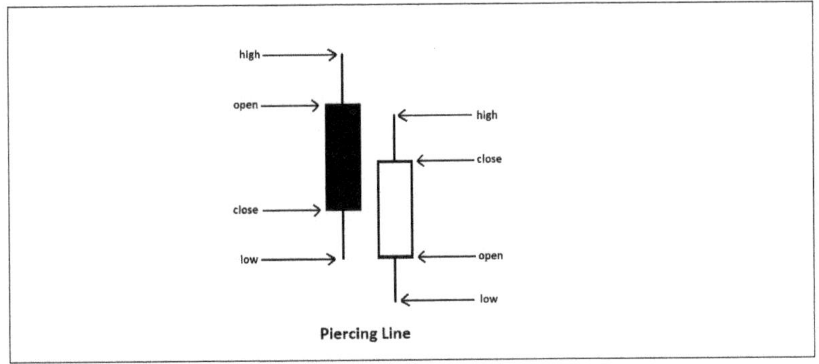

figure 9.34

A bullish candle that pierces the previous bearish candle is interpreted as a sign of bullish strength and a possible shift in sentiment. That may indicate a possible trend reversal, with buyers potentially moving in to push prices higher following a prolonged downturn as shown in *figure 9.35 which* shows how selling is outnumbering buyers at the point where a piercing line pattern forms, followed by price rejection.

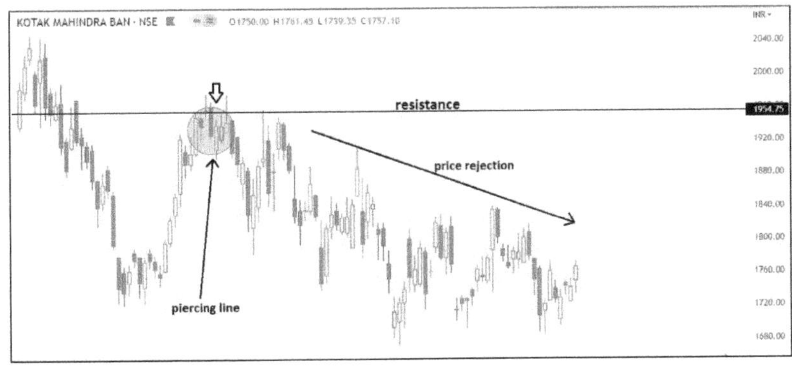

figure 9.35

8. Dark Cloud Line:-

A potential trend reversal may be indicated by the bearish reversal candlestick pattern known as the black cloud cover. It appears near the end of an upswing and is made up of two candles. The first candle is a massive bullish candle, which is followed by a smaller bearish candle that "covers" more than halfway into the previous bullish candle's body, as shown in *figure 9.36* below:-

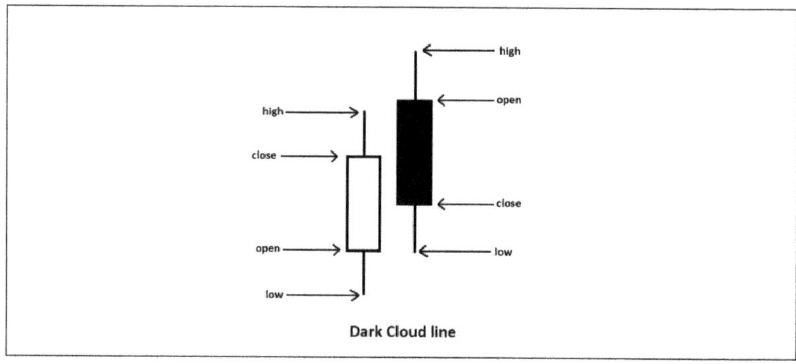

figure 9.36

The heavy cloud cover pattern shows that the bulls are losing control of the market and that the bears are gaining pace.

It can be a warning sign for traders that a trend reversal or downturn is on the way.

The negative candle that covers the previous bullish candle is interpreted as an indication of bearish strength and a potential shift in sentiment as shown in *figure 9.37* on the next page.

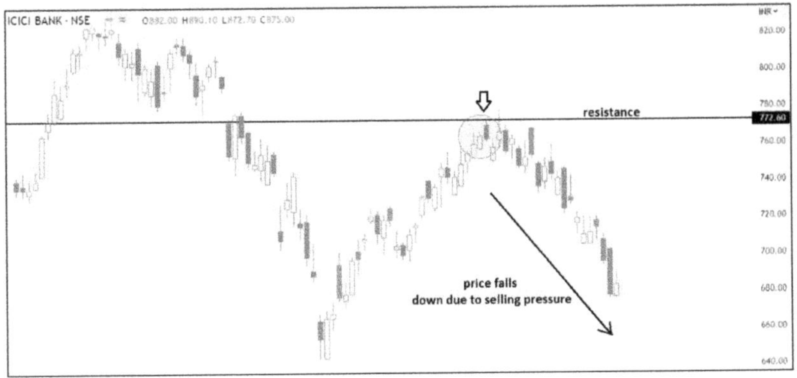

figure 9.37

9. Tweezer Bottom:-

It is formed at the end of a decline by two or more candlesticks with matching lows as shown in *figure 9.38*. The tweezer bottom pattern indicates that the bears are losing momentum while the bulls are gaining power. The tweezer bottom is a bullish reversal candlestick pattern that might indicate a possible trend change.

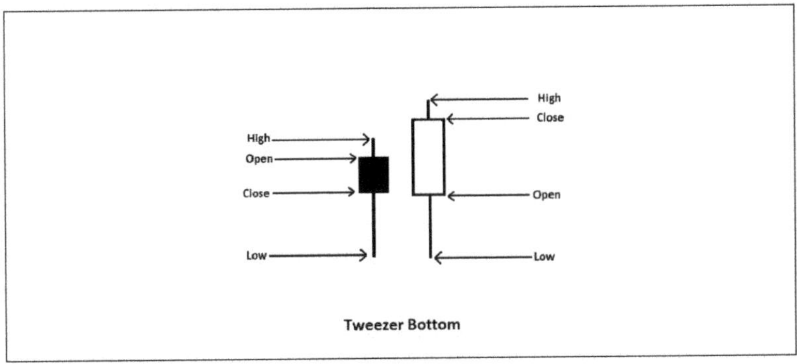

figure 9.38

A bearish candlestick is frequently followed by a bullish candlestick with the same or very similar low as the preceding bearish candlestick to form the tweezer bottom pattern. The overlapping lows form a "tweezer" or "double bottom," indicating that the price has found support at that level. This can be a bullish indicator since it indicates that the bears were unable to push the price lower and that the bulls may now take control. This can be seen in *figure 9.39* where, after forming of tweezer bottom pattern a bullish movement can be seen due to buying pressure.

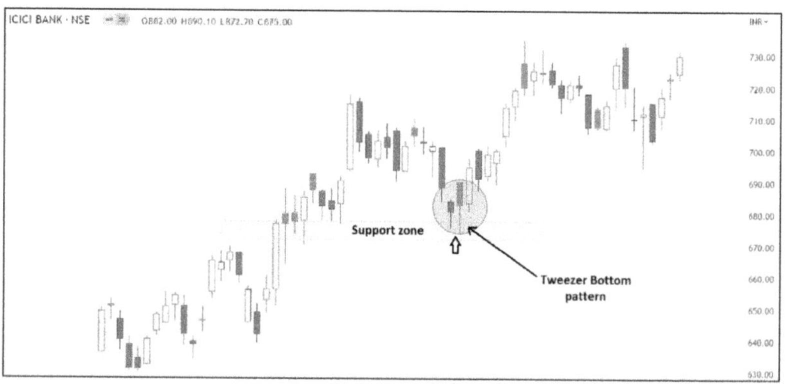

figure 9.39

10. Tweezer top:-

This pattern is formed by two candlesticks that have the same high price. The first candlestick is a bullish candlestick, signifying a bullish mood. It opens at a low price and closes at a high price. The second candlestick is a bearish candlestick, reflecting a bearish mood. It opens near the same high price as the first candlestick and finishes near the low price so it is a bearish reversal pattern that typically forms at the top of an uptrend. this can be seen in *figure 9.40* below:-

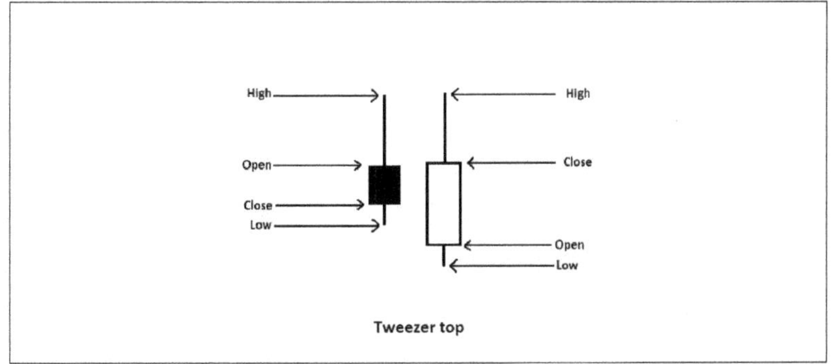

figure 9.40

Figure 9.41 shows the formation of a tweezer top and what occurs if it forms near a resistance zone.

Figure 9.41

Here in *figure 9.41*, you can see firstly there was an uptrend in which sellers as not present but at the resistance, zone sellers are dominating buyers and hence they form a tweezer top pattern which is bearish due to this price started falling suddenly due to selling pressure

Triple candlestick pattern

Three successive candlesticks on a price chart generate these patterns. They are employed in technical analysis to forecast the direction of an asset's price movement. There are various types of triple candlestick patterns, each with its unique interpretation. Some of them are discussed below:-

- Three White Soldiers
- Three Black crows
- Three inside up
- Three inside down
- Morning Star
- Evening Star

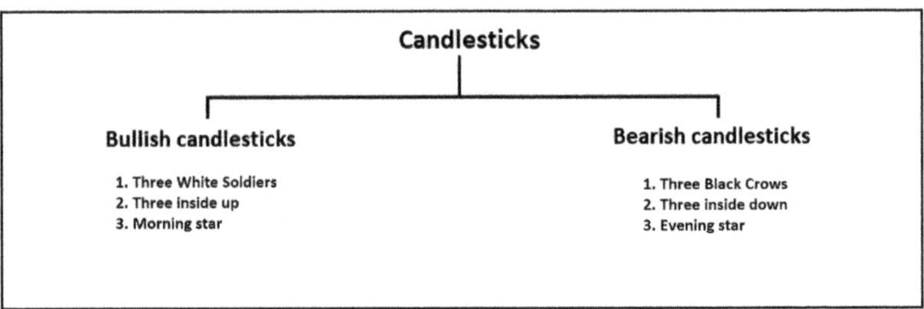

1. Three White Soldiers:-

Three consecutive bullish white or green candlesticks form this pattern. Throughout the pattern, each candlestick begins higher than the previous day's closing and closes near its high, signaling strong buying pressure. The three candles must be lengthy and have extremely small top shadows. as shown in *figure 9.42* below:-

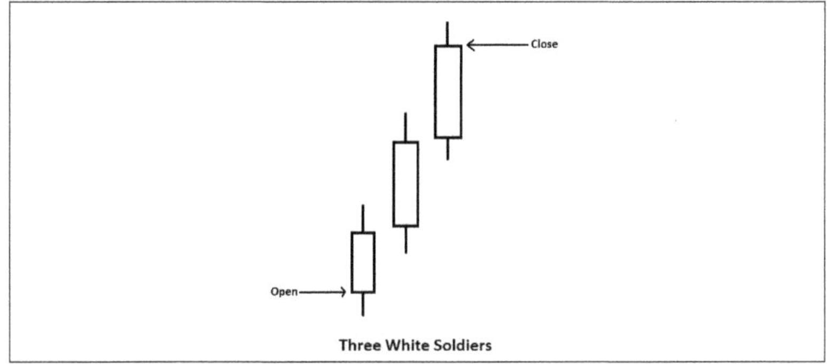

figure 9.42

Now we will examine a graphical representation of this pattern and what happens to the stock as a result of it. *Figure 9.43* I utilized the Nifty Bank chart in the 1 day timeframe, and it can be observed that three white soldiers formed on the chart as a result of purchasing pressure, and the stock price then turned from a downtrend to an uptrend.

Figure 9.43

2. Three Black Crows:-

This pattern is totally opposite to the three white crows pattern, It is only generated at the end of an uptrend when three consecutive bearish candlesticks open within the previous candle's genuine body and form lower close prices, suggesting a strong downward trend. Each should have a long body with little to no existing shadow, indicating that the price is being pushed down by the bears It can be seen in *figure 9.44:-*

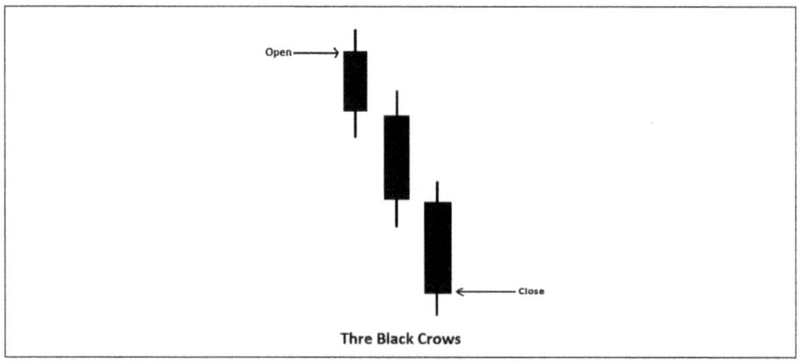

figure 9.44

In *figure 9.45* on the next page, I have used MRF LTD on 1-day time frame in which, we can see that a three-black crows pattern formed around resistance, causing the stock price to fall and the trend to alter.

Here, sellers exceed buyers, and thus the trend becomes bearish.

figure 9.45

3. Three Inside Up:-

After a decline, a bullish reversal pattern known as the "inside up" candlestick pattern appears. It consists of two candlesticks, with the second candlestick falling between the previous candlestick's high and low ranges.

The first candlestick is a bearish candlestick that comes during a drop, indicating the presence of selling pressure.

It has a higher peak and a lower low than the previous candlestick. The second candlestick, which occurs quickly after the first, is a bullish candlestick.

It opens within the high and low ranges of the preceding candlestick and then closes above the first candlestick's high, indicating a potential downtrend reversal. this can be seen in *figure 9.46 :-*

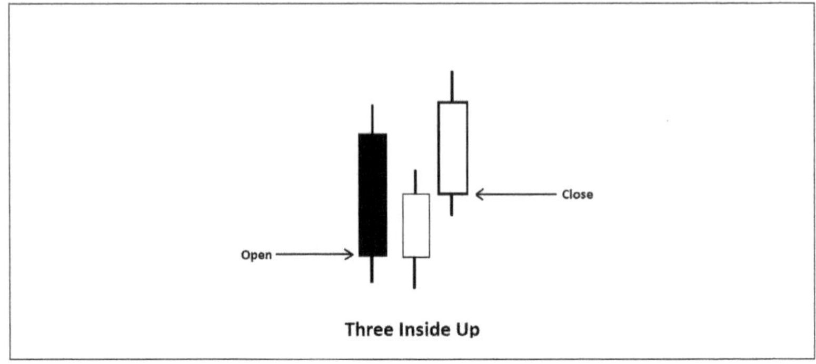

figure 9.46

After the preceding selling pressure, this candlestick pattern indicates that buyers are gathering momentum and seizing control. It can signal a possible trend reversal to an uptrend, which traders may interpret as a signal to initiate long holdings or exit short positions. In *figure 9.47*, I utilized the Eicher Motors chart in the 1-day timeframe. An inside-up pattern can be observed established on the support level, followed by bullish momentum, and the stock price rises.

figure 9.47

4. *Three inside down:-*

The "three inside down" candlestick pattern is a bearish reversal pattern that appears following an uptrend. It is made up of three successive candlesticks and is seen as a negative indication of a possible trend reversal. The three inside down pattern is produced as follows:

The **first candlestick** is a bullish candlestick that appears during an uptrend, signaling that buying pressure is present. It has a higher high and lower low than the previous candlestick. The **second candlestick** is a bearish candlestick It opens above the first candlestick's high but finishes below the first candlestick's low, totally engulfing the first candlestick's range. The **third candlestick** confirms the possible trend reversal by closing lower than the second candlestick, extending the bearish momentum, this pattern can be seen in *figure 9.48* below:-

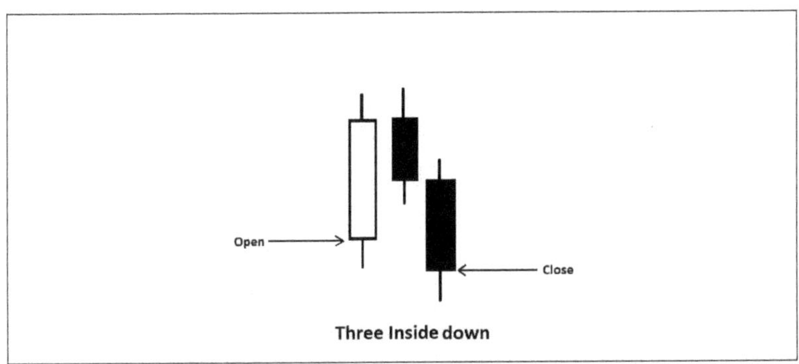

figure 9.48

It suggests that sellers have regained control and are reversing the previous uptrend. Traders may perceive it as a signal to enter short positions or exit long positions. In below *figure 9.49*, I used an IndusInd Bank chart with a one-day time frame. Inner down pattern produced on the resistance level, from where sellers entered the market and caused the price to decline.

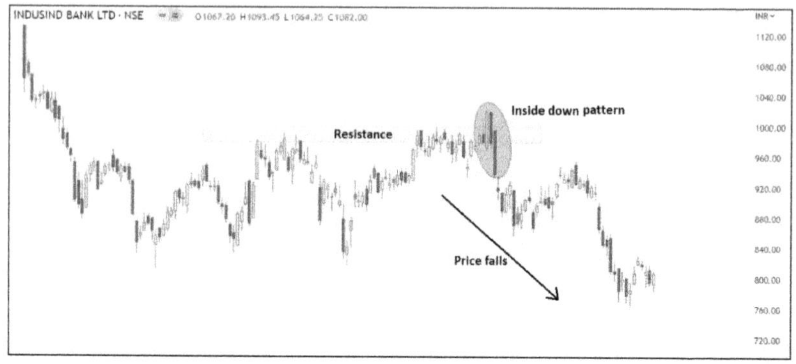

figure 9.49

5. Morning Star:-

The morning star pattern indicates a shift in attitude from pessimistic to bullish, with trading possibilities. It is a reversal situation that developed near the end of a downtrend.

It consists of a first long bearish candle, a second with a smaller body that gaps below the first, and a third bullish candle that closes above the first's midpoint.

This signals that the bears are losing control and that the bulls are gaining control. It can be seen in *figure 9.50* on the next page.

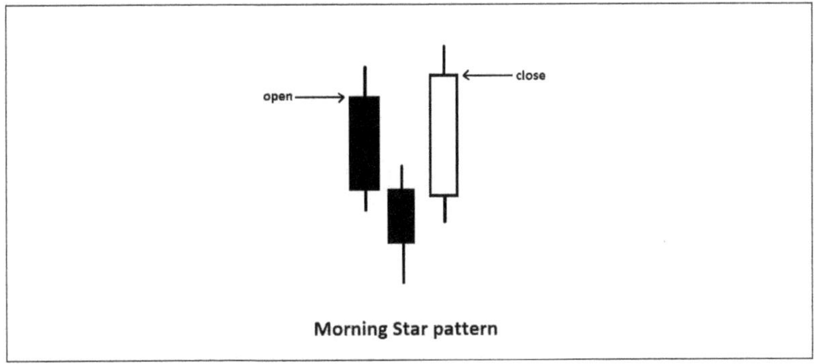

figure 9.50

The formation of the morning star pattern in the graph can be observed in *figure 9.51*, where I used the Ethereum chart for 1 hour period and it can be seen that after the formation of the morning star pattern on resistance, a reversal occurs, and price rises due to buying pressure.

figure 9.51

6. Evening Star:-

This reversal setup formed at the end of an uptrend is the evening star. It is totally opposite to the morning star pattern. It consists of a first long bullish candle, a second (bullish or bearish) candle with a smaller body that may gap over the preceding, indicating that the trend has not yet been determined, and a third bearish candle, closing at least within the body of the first. It can be seen in *figure 9.52*. This suggests that the bulls are losing control and the bears are gaining control, implying a possible reversal of the present upswing.

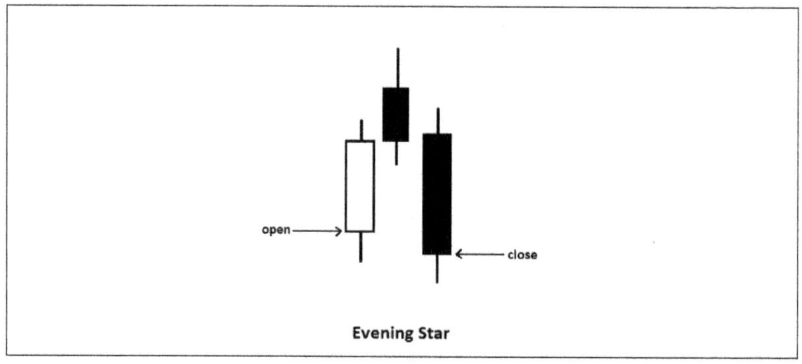

figure 9.52

Figure 9.53depicts the creation of an Evening star pattern. I used the UPL LTD chart on the 1-day time frame, and a price reversal setup occurred on resistance after the construction of an evening star pattern. But, like with any trading pattern, other factors such as market background, and trend strength.

UPL LTD · NSE   O725.05 H729.85 L725.05 C728.90
INR
804.00
800.00
796.00
792.15
788.00
784.00
780.00
776.00
772.00
768.00
764.00
760.00
756.00
752.00
resisitance
Evening star
price pullback

Figure 9.53

IX

Formation of a New Candlestick

How to combine candlesticks to form a new candlestick?

We've seen numerous candlesticks and their many types and patterns, but do you know how such patterns can be accomplished in a single candlestick? Thus, in this chapter, we'll talk about how to combine those candles to build a new candlestick and determine if it's a bullish or bearish candlestick in a higher time frame. It will help to provide you clarity.

Steps to combine candlesticks

Let's say you have 2 candles as shown in *figure 10.1*

1. Mark the "opening" point of 1ˢᵗ candle (it can be any bullish or bearish).
2. Now similarly mark the "closing" point of the second candle (bullish or bearish).

3. Also, mark the "Low" and "High" points of the candles as shown in the below figure.

4. After you've marked both points, construct a new one based on the opening and closing points of both that you've recently marked, and its wick by "high" and "low" points.

5. Those two candlesticks will combine to form a new candlestick as shown below.

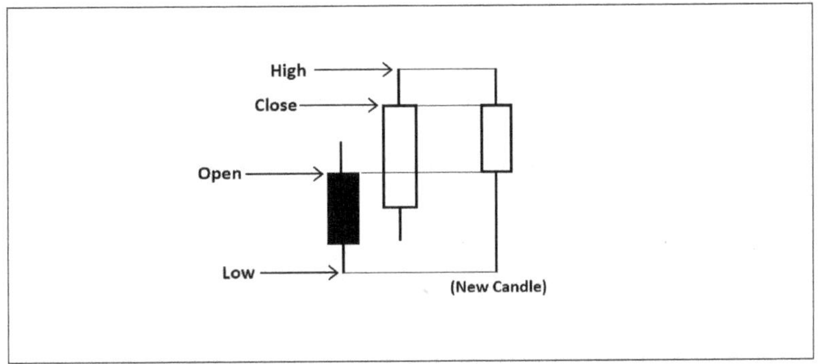

figure 10.1

Let's say now you have 3 candles as shown in *figure 10.2*

1. Mark the "opening" point of 1st candle the same as we have done for two candles (it can be any bullish or bearish).

2. Now similarly mark the "closing" point of the last candle (bullish or bearish).

3. Also, mark the "Low" and "High" points of the "first" and "last" candles as shown in the below figure.

4. After you've marked both points, construct a new one based on the opening and closing points of both that you've recently marked, and its wick by marking the "high" and "low" points of the first and last candle as shown in the figure below.

5. Those Three candlesticks will combine to form a new candlestick as shown.

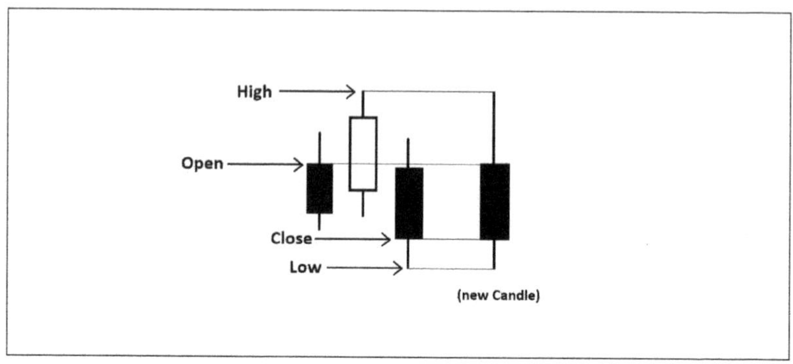

figure 10.2

<u>Note:-This process can be applied to as many candles as you wish.</u>

X

Breakout, Retest and Confirmation

What is Breakout?

A breakout is defined as a price movement of a stock or commodity above an established level of resistance or support, which is frequently accompanied by high volumes and higher volatility. Breakouts can occur in a variety of market situations and timeframes, as well as in numerous chart patterns such as double top/bottom, head, and shoulders, cup and holder, etc.

A breakout can occur on the upside if the price rises above a resistance level, indicating a potential bullish indication, or on the downside if the price falls below a support level, indicating a potential bearish signal. Traders buy stocks or commodities when the price rises above a specific level of resistance, and sell when the price falls below a given level of support.

Figure 10.1 shows that how a breakout appears above resistance, below support :

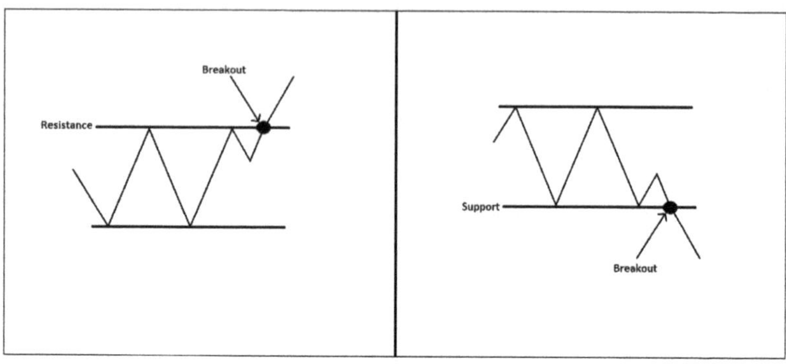

figure 10.1

What is Fake Breakout?

When a price moves through an indicated level of support or resistance but lacks the momentum to continue in that direction and comes back to the level of breakout. When the price of an asset moves above or below the pattern or range.

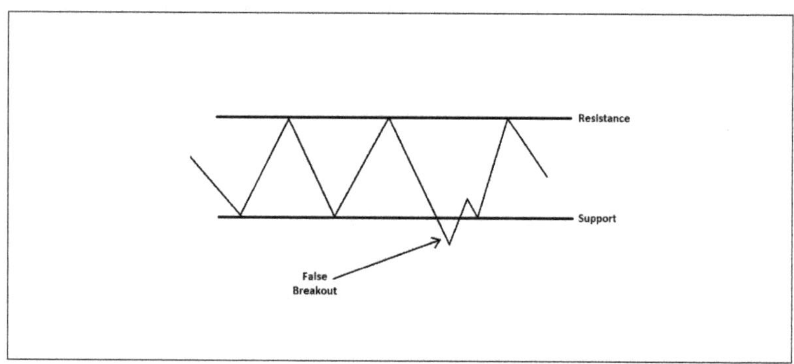

Figure 10.2

Figure 10.2 shows you how a fake breakout looks like. It indicates a probable trend continuation or reversal, and in some cases, the breakout may not be genuine and may result in a fake breakout.

<u>Some reasons for a fake breakout are given below</u>:-

1. Market volatility
2. False signals from the indicators
3. News or events
4. Lack of volumes of buying and selling

<u>How to avoid fake Breakouts</u>:-

1. Use many indication tools in the chart like indicators, trendline, support, and resistance.
2. Use proper Risk management
3. Avoid over trading
4. Always wait for confirmation before entering a trade

What is Retesting?

A retesting is a price movement that returns to a previous level of support or resistance following a breakout or breakdown. If the price successfully retests the breakout or breakdown level and continues to move in the direction of the original breakout or breakdown, it can indicate the strength of the trend.

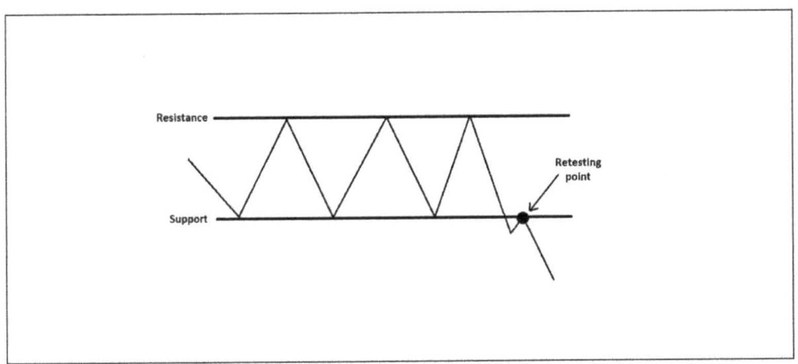

figure 10.3

On the other hand, if the price fails to hold above the breakout or breakdown level during a retest and reverses, it may signify a potential false breakout or breakdown, and traders may need to reevaluate their trading strategy. *Figure 10.3* above shows you the retesting point.

Retests can provide an opportunity to initiate a trade with a higher risk-reward ratio, as traders can set stop-loss orders below the breakout or breakdown level in the event that the retest fails and the price reverses. Retest analysis, when combined with other technical and fundamental factors, can assist traders in making better-informed trading decisions.

What is Confirmation?

The process of validating a trading signal or pattern with some candlestick pattern, additional indicators, analysis, or criteria in order to maximize the likelihood of a successful transaction. Confirmations assist traders in reducing erroneous signals and making better trading decisions.

Confirmation can depend on any of the following points:

1. Using Candlestick type: If you are looking to trade bullish on any of the patterns and suddenly as a green signal a bullish hammer or a bullish engulfing candle forms around the support or trendline, it can be a nice bullish confirmation for you as in *figure 10.4*. I utilized the HDFC Life Insurance chart on a one-day time frame, and following bullish momentum, it forms a trendline, and after the breakout, a large bullish candle forms, which is a solid sign to confirm the bullish trend.

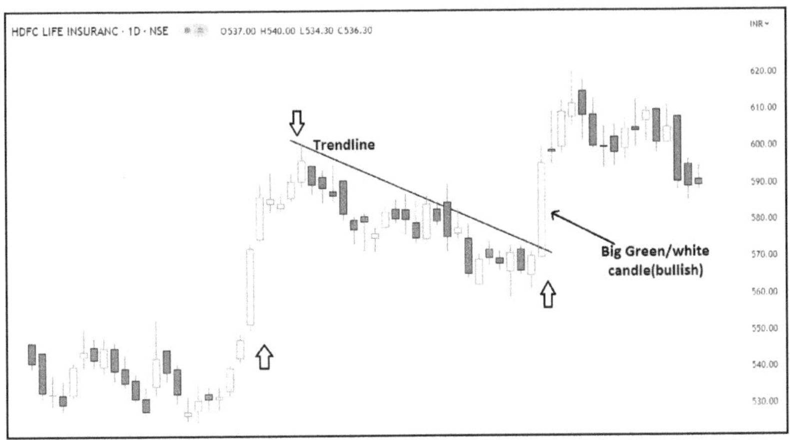

figure 10.4

2. <u>By trading signal or pattern</u>: This could be a chart pattern, a price level, or any other type of indicator that indicates a possible trading opportunity.

Assume you examined a pattern that is emerging in the chart; now you will draw it and wait for the breakout point to check that it will work on behalf of the pattern.

Like on the next page in *figure 10.5,* I utilized the HDFC Life Insurance chart on a 4-hour time frame, and you can see that after consolidation, it forms a rectangular pattern that is neutral in behavior.

It gave a breakout on the positive side, confirming that the upcoming trend is bullish.

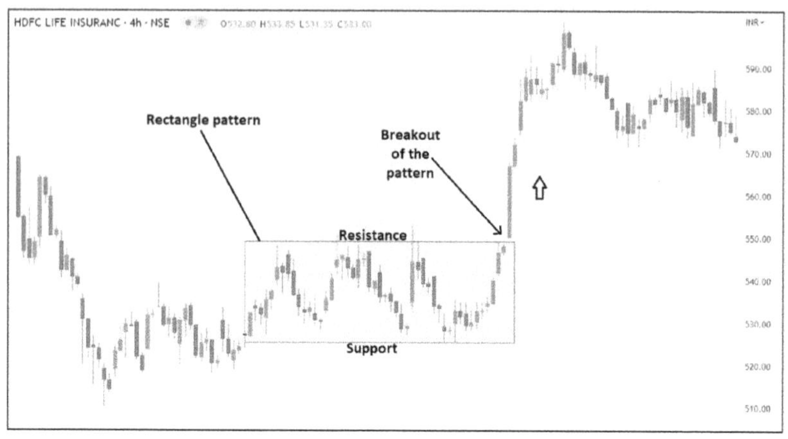

figure 10.5

3. <u>Using indicators</u>: To validate the first signal or pattern, use other technical indicators, chart patterns, or tools.

Using several periods, different types of indicators, or testing for confluence with other technical levels, such as support and resistance zones, could all be examples of this or you can use other technical indicators like moving averages.

On the next page i have shown in *figure 10.6 in* which Bajaj Finance LTD chart on 1-day time frame in which the price takes support on the moving average line and then breaks through it, indicating the confirmation of a bullish trend.

BAJAJ FINANCE LTD · 1D · NSE   O 5998.00 H 5998.00 L 5900.00 C 5931.30
EMA 50 close 0 SMA 9   5952.36
Moving Average
(indicator)
Price taking support
on ema line

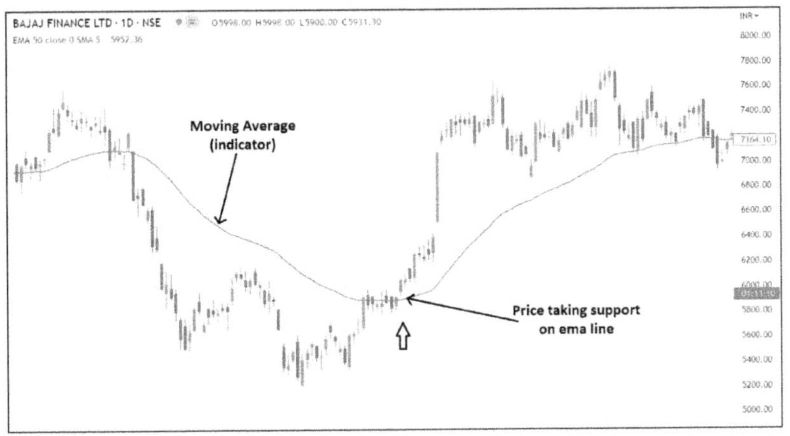

figure 10.6

XI

Candlestick chart patterns

What are Candlestick Chart Patterns?

Trade patterns are recurrent shapes or combinations on price charts that provide information about future price movements. Traders employ these patterns as part of technical analysis, which is a method of forecasting future price movements by evaluating historical price data.

Trade patterns can be seen in various periods, ranging from intraday charts to daily, weekly, or monthly charts. These patterns are used by traders to discover prospective trading opportunities, make buy/sell choices, set stop-loss and take-profit levels, and manage market risk. Trading patterns are founded on the assumption that price movements in the past tend to repeat themselves, as human psychology and market dynamics frequently result in similar patterns forming over time. Traders strive to get an advantage in predicting future price fluctuations and making lucrative trading decisions by recognizing and comprehending these patterns.

To validate signals and make informed trading decisions, traders employ trading patterns in conjunction with other technical analysis tools like trendlines, support, and resistance levels, moving averages, and indicators. It is crucial to remember that trading patterns are not failsafe. It should be utilized with adequate risk management and consideration of other pertinent elements such as fundamental research, market mood, and news events as part of a holistic trading strategy.

There are three types of Candlestick chart patterns:-

1. Reversal chart patterns
2. Neutral chart patterns
3. Continuous chart patterns

Now we will discuss them all one by one:-

1. Reversal chart patterns:

These types of charts suggest a likely price trend reversal in the opposite direction. These patterns can be seen on price charts and alert traders when a trend is ending and a new trend is beginning in the opposite direction and provide valuable insights to traders and can be used as part of a comprehensive trading strategy to identify potential trading opportunities and manage risks effectively.

some famous reversal chart patterns are given below:-

- Double top
- Double bottom
- Triple top
- Triple bottom
- Head and shoulders
- Inverted Head and shoulders
- Rounding top
- Rounding bottom

<u>Double top</u>: It is a bearish pattern that may imply a market reversal for a period of time. It denotes a trend reversal from up to down. It suggests that buying pressure has diminished and that sellers are gaining control.

The pattern is often composed of two peaks that are roughly at the same level, followed by a trough or valley in between that serves as a support level known as the neckline. Furthermore, the Target is located below the neckline(support), up to the point illustrated in the picture. *Figure 11.1* shows you what a double-top pattern looks like.

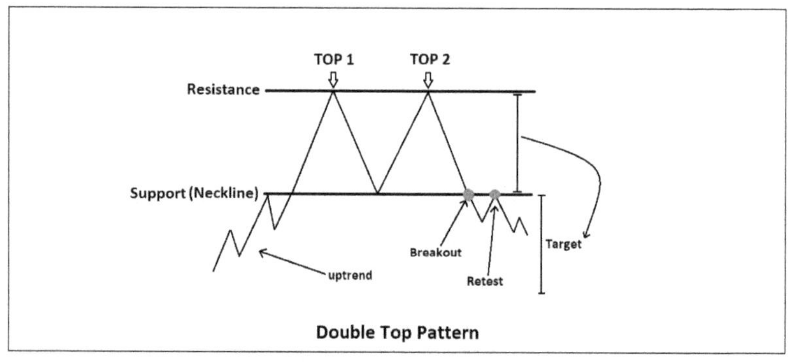

figure 11.1

When the price of an asset is trapped between the support and resistance levels and reaches two peaks on the resistance level, the price declines slightly and breaks the price level of support, as shown in Figure 11.1. Furthermore, the Target is located below the neckline(support), up to the point illustrated in the picture.

On the next page, in *figure 11.2*, you'll see how it looks in an actual chart. In that figure, I used the Mahindra & Mahindra chart on a one-day time frame, and the formation of a double top pattern is visible.

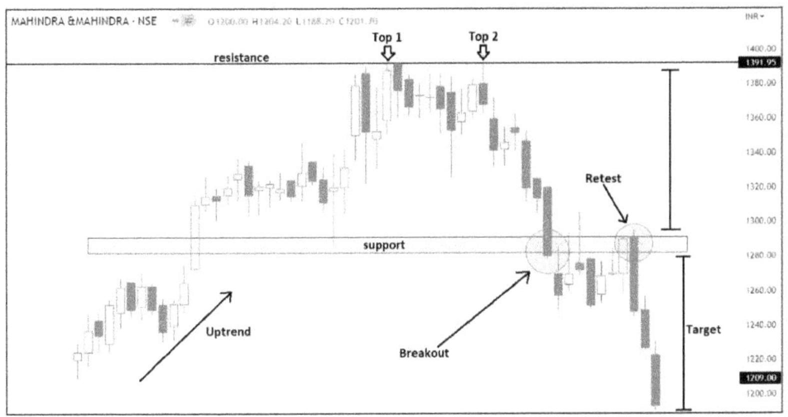

figure 11.2

The double-top pattern is not perfect and can create false signals sometimes. Traders should look for bearish candlestick patterns near the second high, such as shooting stars or bearish engulfing patterns, for confirmation. To limit the risks involved with trading based on the double top pattern, they can apply risk management tactics such as setting stop-loss orders and controlling position sizing.

<u>Double bottom</u>: It is opposite of the double top pattern. It is a bullish reversal pattern that may imply a market reversal for a period of time. It denotes a trend reversal from down to up. It suggests that selling pressure has diminished and that buyers are gaining control.

It is made up of two troughs or valleys that are roughly at the same level, generating two "bottoms" on the price chart, with a peak or rally in between, known as the "neckline." When the price finds support at the troughs and resistance at the neckline, the pattern is formed. This pattern can be seen in *figure 11.3* on the next page:

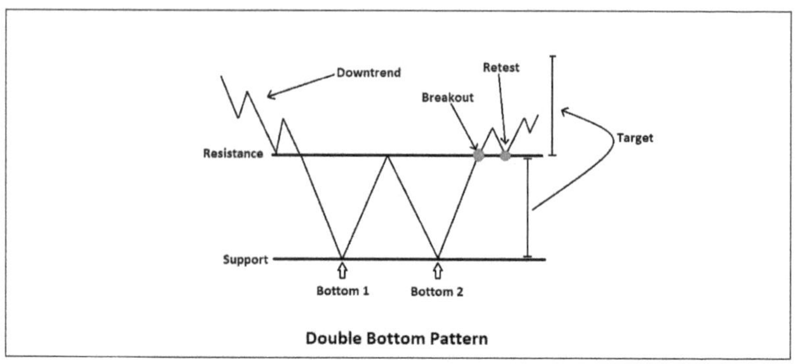

figure 11.3

Normally, volume is larger during the troughs than at the peak, indicating stronger purchasing interest and potential bullish momentum during the troughs. *Figure 11.4* shows how a double bottom pattern appears in the graph. I utilized the Tata Power chart in one of the weak time frames where the formation of a double bottom pattern can be easily seen.

Figure 11.4

Triple top: It is a bearish reversal pattern that consists of three peaks at or on the resistance level, indicating a likely uptrend reversal and a possible decline ahead as shown in *figure 11.5*

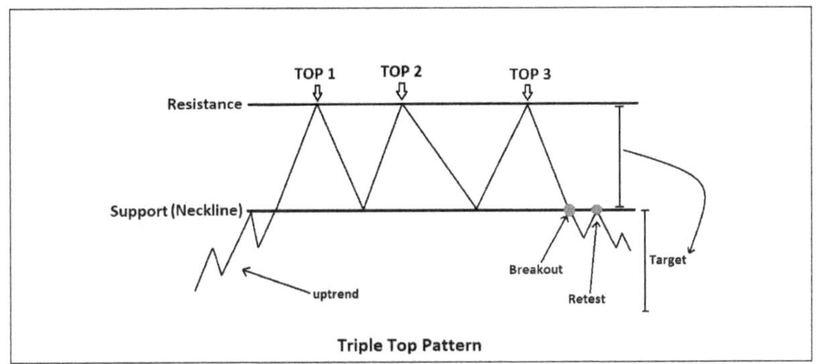

figure 11.5

The following are the primary elements of a Triple Top pattern:

- <u>After an uptrend</u>: The Triple Top pattern often emerges after a prolonged uptrend, signaling that the market's bullish impetus is fading.
- <u>Three top levels</u>: The pattern is made up of three peaks that are roughly at the same level and form resistance. These peaks are typically separated by troughs or valleys, resulting in support levels.
- <u>Neckline:</u> The neckline is a trendline that runs across the troughs or valleys connecting the three peaks. It serves as a level of assistance. A breakdown below the neckline confirms the Triple Top pattern and may indicate a potential trend reversal.
- <u>Bearish reversal:</u> The Triple Top pattern is a bearish reversal pattern, indicating that the price may reverse from an uptrend to a downturn. If the pattern is confirmed, traders may search for short-selling opportunities or contemplate exiting long positions.

Now, a graphical representation of this pattern is provided below (figure 11.6) so you can see how it appears in the original chart. I selected an Infosys LTD chart on a 1-hour timeframe so you could see how it formed.

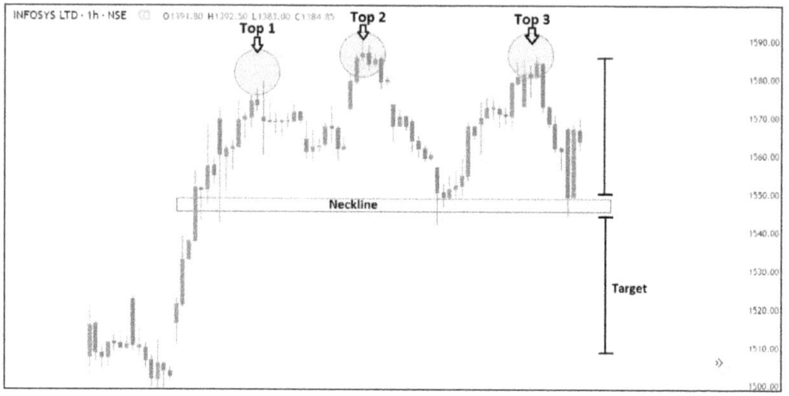

figure 11.6

<u>Triple bottom</u>: Triple bottom is totally opposite of the triple top chart pattern. It is a bullish reversal pattern that indicates a possible trend reversal from a downtrend to an uptrend.

After the sellers failed to break the support in three consecutive attempts, this candlestick pattern implies an upcoming change in trend direction.

The pattern often occurs after a prolonged downtrend and comprises three bottoms at roughly the same level, separated by two peaks, resulting in a pattern that resembles three consecutive bottoms as shown in *figure 11.7* on the next page.

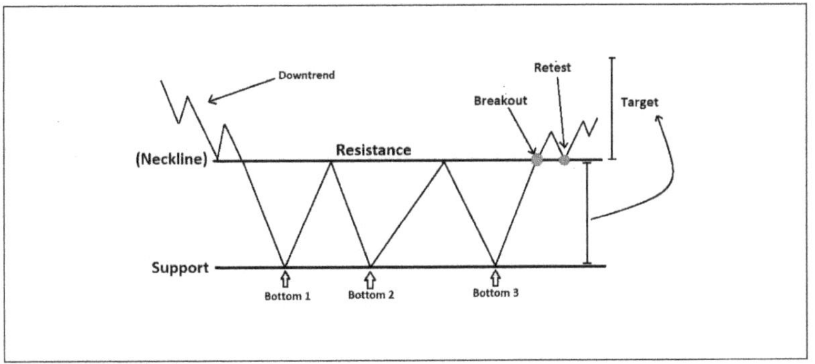

figure 11.7

The following are the primary elements of a Triple Bottom pattern:

- <u>After a downtrend:</u> The Triple Bottom pattern often emerges after a prolonged decline, signaling that the market's bearish momentum is fading.
- <u>Three bottom levels:</u> The pattern is made up of three troughs that are roughly at the same level and form support. These troughs are typically separated by peaks, resulting in resistance levels.
- <u>The neckline:</u> The neckline is a trendline that is drawn between the peaks connecting the three troughs. It serves as a level of resistance. A break above the neckline confirms the Triple Bottom pattern and may indicate a potential trend reversal.
- <u>Bullish reversal:</u> The Triple Bottom pattern is a bullish reversal pattern, indicating that the price may revert from a downtrend to an uptrend. If the pattern is confirmed, traders may search for buying opportunities or consider exiting short holdings.

On the next page in *figure 11.8* Bharat Electronics chart is shown on a 1-day time frame so, you can see how the triple bottom pattern appears in the original candlestick chart. You can clearly observe that due to significant selling pressure, the downtrend is continuing on bottom 1, and the price takes support three times in a row on the same support zone, forming a triple bottom pattern.

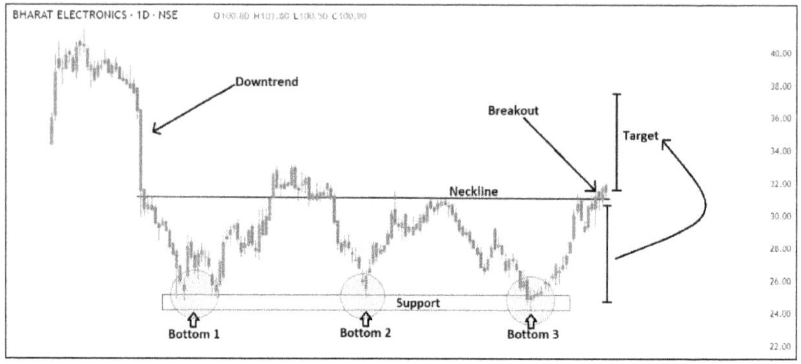

figure 11.8

Head and shoulders: What comes to mind when you read the name of this chart is probably the shampoo brand, but this isn't related to that. Now let me explain, It is a reversal pattern that is commonly seen as an indication of a trend reversal from bullish to bearish.

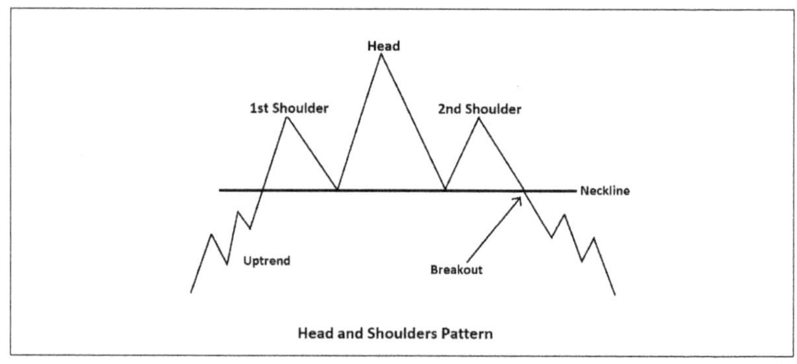

figure 11.9

A left shoulder, a head, and a right shoulder are the three major components of the head and shoulders pattern. These elements combine to generate a visual pattern that resembles a human head and shoulders. *Figure 11.9* shows you how a Head and Shoulders pattern looks like.

On a candlestick chart, the head and shoulders pattern is often identified as follows:

- <u>Left Shoulders:</u> The pattern begins with an upswing in which prices are generally rising. A higher high followed by a pullback forms the left shoulder, resulting in a tiny peak on the chart.
- <u>Head:</u> After the left shoulder, prices rally once again, reaching a higher peak than the left shoulder. This higher high is known as the pattern's head and is usually the highest point in the pattern.
- <u>Right Shoulder:</u> Following the head, prices pull back, generating another tiny high that is usually lower than the head. This is the pattern's right shoulder.
- <u>Neckline:</u> The neckline is a trendline formed by linking the low points of the pullbacks from the left shoulder, head, and right shoulder. It serves as a level of support for the pattern.

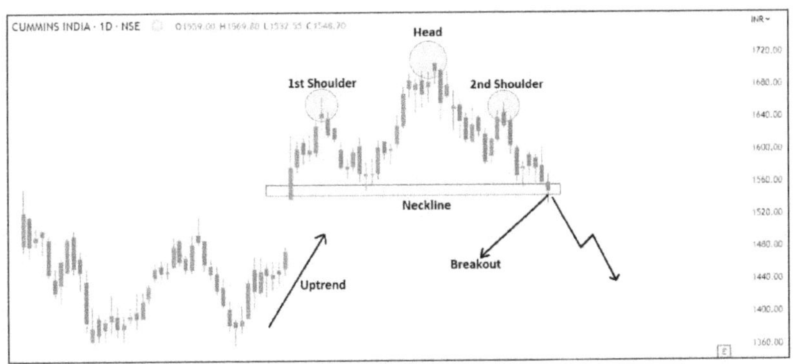

figure 11.10

As shown in *Figure 11.10*, there is a significant difference between a real candlestick graph and the theoretical graph*(figure 11.9)*.

If found, traders may view the pattern as a probable bearish reversal signal. A collapse below the neckline following the formation of the right shoulder is sometimes regarded as a confirmation of the pattern, signaling that the uptrend may be reversing and prices may begin to fall. When the pattern is verified, traders may search for short-selling opportunities or contemplate leaving long positions.

<u>Inverted Head and shoulders</u>: An inverted head and shoulders pattern is the inverse of a standard head and shoulders pattern and is a common chart pattern in technical analysis.

It is a bullish reversal pattern that is commonly recognized as an indication of a trend reversal from bearish to positive.

This pattern like the last one also has three distinct features: a left shoulder, a head, and a right shoulder are the three major components of the head and shoulders pattern. A Head and Shoulders design is depicted in *Figure 11.9* :

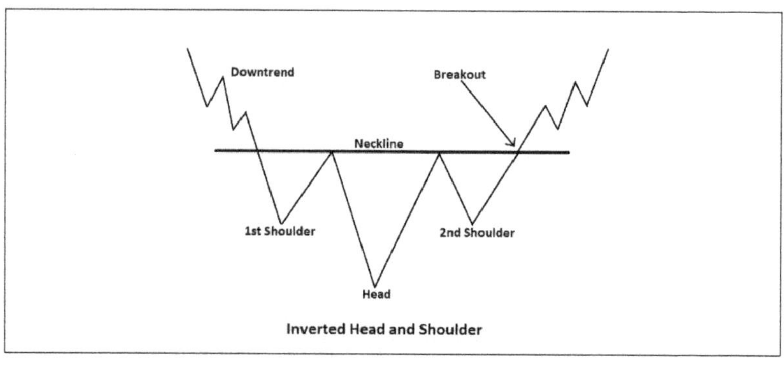

figure 11.11

On a candlestick chart, the inverted head and shoulders pattern is often identified as follows:

- <u>Left Shoulder:</u> The pattern begins with a downtrend in which prices are generally dropping. A lower low followed by a rebound forms the left shoulder, resulting in a tiny trough on the chart.
- <u>Head:</u> After the left shoulder, prices fall again, establishing a lower low than the left shoulder. Its lower low is known as the pattern's head and is usually the lowest point in the pattern.
- <u>Right Shoulder:</u> Following the head, prices rebound, generating another tiny trough that is usually higher than the head. This is the pattern's right shoulder.
- <u>Neckline:</u> A trendline formed by linking the high points of the rebounds between the left shoulder, head, and right shoulder is known as the neckline. It serves as a level of resistance to the pattern.

As shown in *Figure 11.12* on the next page I have shown you the graph of US dollar/ Japanese Yen on a 1-hour time frame you can clearly see the inverted head and shoulder pattern this is what an actual head and shoulders pattern looks like in a real candlestick chart.

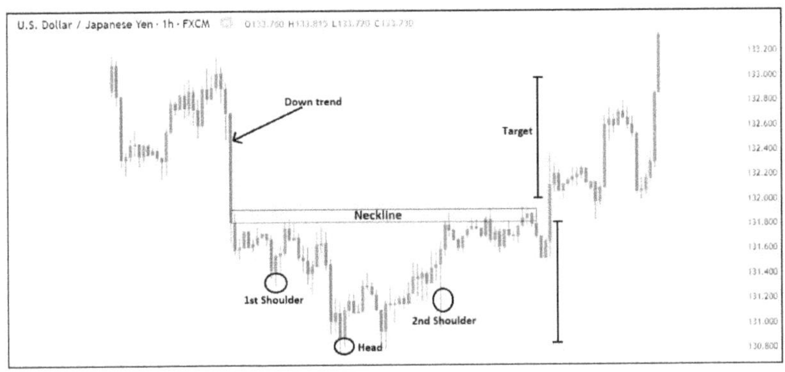

figure 11.12

<u>Rounding top</u>: On a price chart, the rounding top pattern is distinguished by a curved or semi-circular shape in which the price advances in a series of higher highs and higher lows, forming a rounded shape as shown in *figure 11.13*. It is also known as an "inverted saucer" or "topping shape."It is usually thought to be a long-term pattern that can take weeks or even months to emerge.

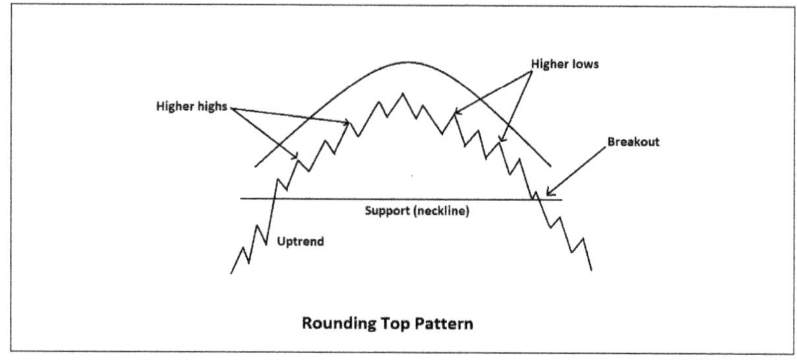

figure 11.13

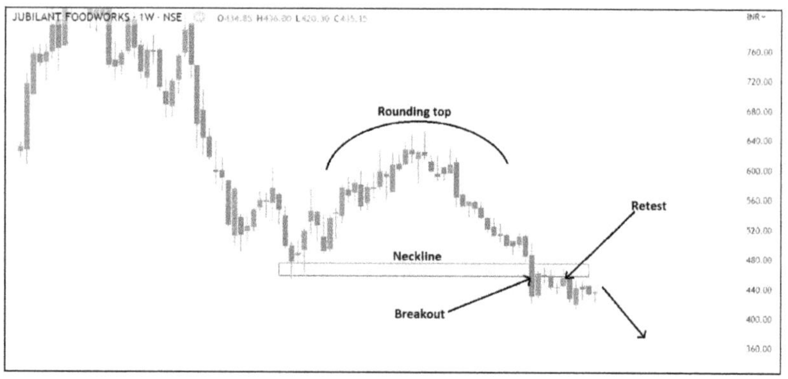

figure 11.14

In *figure 11.14* you can see the graphical chart of bajaj finance forming proper rounding top pattern.

As the price fails to hit new highs and begins to flatten or round off, the rounding top pattern is generally viewed as a sign of waning bullish momentum. That could imply that purchasing pressure is receding while selling pressure is building, potentially leading to a trend reversal. Before making trading decisions, traders and investors should look for other technical indicators or confirmation signals to validate the rounded top pattern.

Rounding bottom: It is opposite of rounding top pattern and also known as saucer bottom. It is a bullish reversal chart pattern that can suggest a possible trend change from a downtrend to an uptrend.

It is often created over time and is distinguished by a gradual, rounded shape resembling a saucer or a U-shape as shown in *figure 11.15.*

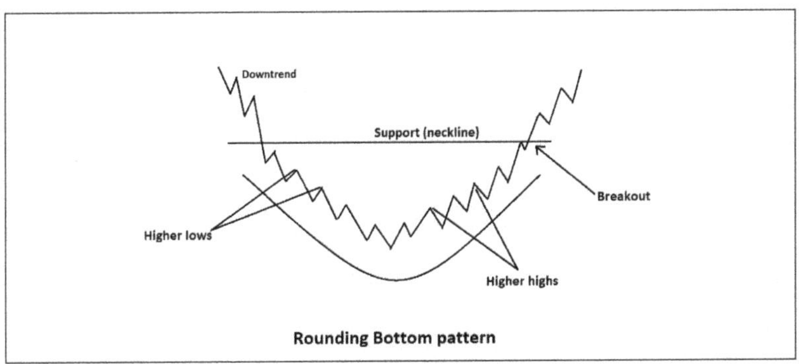

figure 11.15

The bottom of the U-shaped curve represents the lowest point of the downtrend. The rounded bottom pattern is verified when prices break above a neckline, which is a horizontal line drawn across the pattern's highs, as seen in figure 11.16. As shown in figure, the price target for the rounded bottom pattern is generally computed by adding the pattern's depth to the breakout point above the neckline.

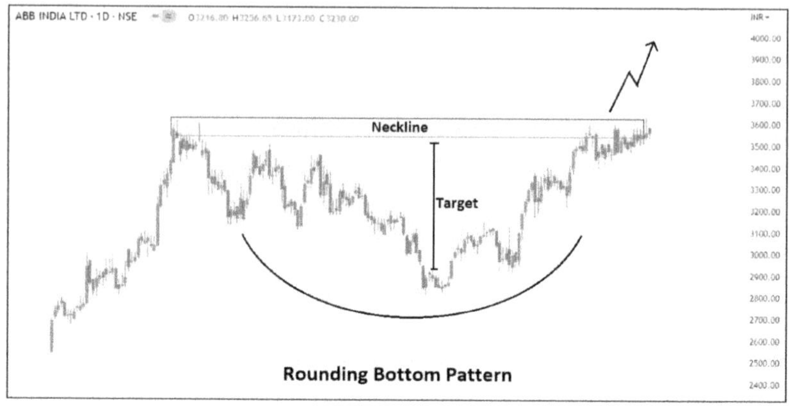

figure 11.16

2. *Neutral chart patterns:*

Neutral chart patterns may not always indicate a clear direction for price movement. These patterns may indicate a time of market consolidation or indecision in which neither buyers nor sellers have a clear advantage. Neutral chart patterns are most common during periods of low volatility or when the market is resting after a big move.

some of the neutral chart patterns are discussed below:-

- Rectangle pattern
- Ascending Triangle
- Descending Triangle
- Symmetrical Triangle
- Rising channel
- Falling channel

Rectangle pattern: When the price of an asset travels inside parallel horizontal trendlines and forms a rectangular shape which is known as a rectangle pattern as shown in *figure 11.17*. It's also known as a trading range or a consolidation pattern.

The rectangle pattern can be spotted by drawing trendlines linking the price movement highs and lows. The top trendline works as a resistance, while the lower trendline provides support. Traders frequently seek a breakout from the rectangle pattern, which could indicate the conclusion of the consolidation phase and the start of a new trend.

There are two types of Rectangle patterns:-

- <u>Bullish Rectangle Pattern</u>: Price tends to break out to the upside in a bullish rectangle formation, indicating a likely bullish trend continuation.
- <u>Bearish Rectangle Pattern:</u> Price tends to break out to the downside in a bearish rectangle pattern, signaling a likely bearish trend continuation.

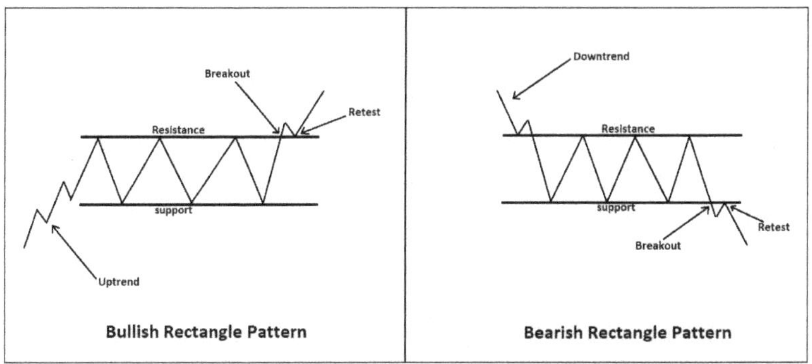

figure 11.17

In *Figure 11.18* I have used the graph of SBI Life Insurance on a weak time frame in which you can simply see that price is consolidating in the rectangle pattern. Whenever it gives a breakout it means sellers entered in the market and they will push the price to the lower side.

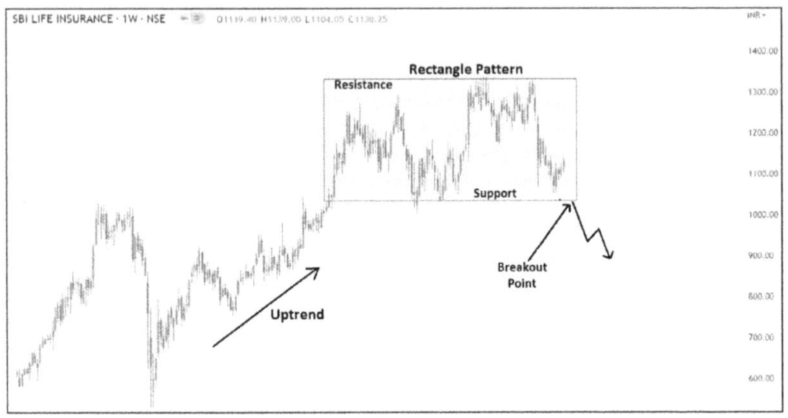

figure 11.18

Triangle Pattern: When the price of an asset converges into a smaller range, The triangle is at its widest point at the start of its formation. As the market continues to trade sideways, the trading range narrows after that a triangular shape appears on a price chart. Triangle patterns can be bullish or bearish depending on how they are oriented in reference to the current trend. It indicates a period of consolidation or indecision in the market.

There are total three types of triangle pattern :-

1. Ascending triangle pattern
2. Descending triangle pattern
3. Symmetrical triangle pattern

Ascending Triangle Pattern: When the price movement makes a horizontal resistance level (upper trendline) and an upward-sloping support level (lower trendline), it forms an ascending triangle pattern, as shown in *figure 11.19*, or we can say that the price makes higher lows, indicating that buyers are becoming more aggressive, while the triangle's upper limit remains relatively flat, indicating that resistance at the upper trendline is phased. This pattern suggests that buyers are gaining strength and a bullish breakout is possible.

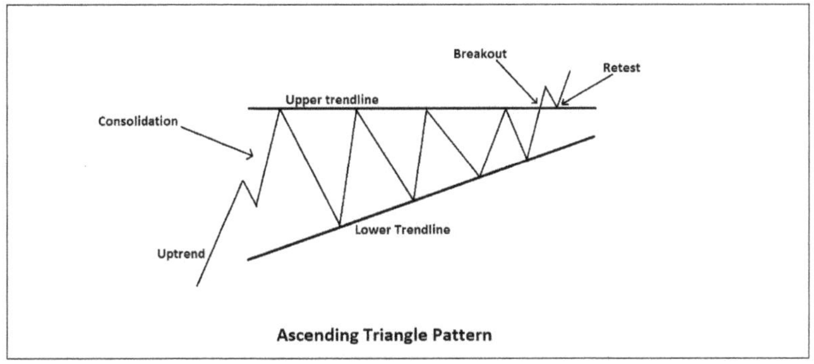

figure 11.19

Traders often look for an ascending triangle pattern as a potential signal to buy the asset.

The pattern suggests that the buyers are becoming more aggressive and are willing to buy at higher prices, indicating a potential breakout above the resistance level.

Now, how an ascending triangle pattern looks in a candlestick graph, I have shown *figure 11.20* on the next pagewhich is the chart of HCL Technologies on a weakly time frame after the uptrend the price consolidated in an ascending triangle pattern followed by support and resistance as trendlines and when buyers re-entered the market the price gave breakout and another uptrend continued.

figure 11.20

<u>Descending triangle pattern</u>: When the price makes a horizontal support level (lower trendline) and a downward sloping resistance level (upper trendline), it forms a descending triangle pattern, as seen in figure 11.21, or the price makes lower highs since the triangle's lower border remains relatively flat.

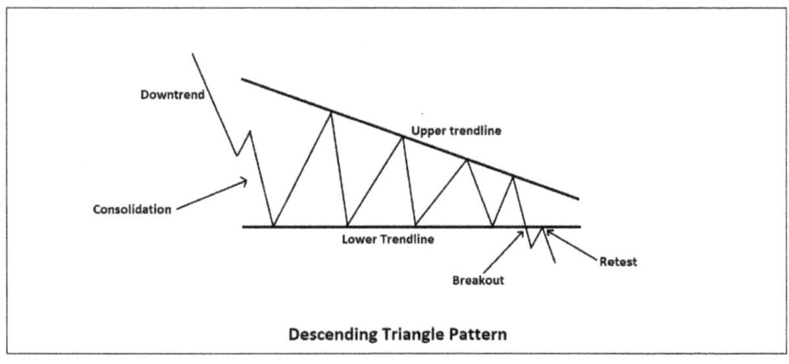

figure 11.21

This could signal that sellers are gradually gaining influence and will eventually drive the price down. Now, how a descending triangle pattern looks in a candlestick graph, I have shown *figure 11.22* which is the chart of Hero Motocorp in 4-hour time frame after the downtrend the price consolidated in a descending triangle pattern followed by support and resistance as upper and lower trendlines and when sellers re-entered the market then price gave breakout and continued the trend.

figure 11.22

<u>Symmetrical triangle pattern:</u> When both the support and resistance trendlines slant towards each other, a symmetrical shape is formed that shape is called a Symmetrical triangle pattern. Lower highs and higher lows are made by the price, signifying a period of indecision and equilibrium between buyers and sellers. This pattern indicates that the market is in an equilibrium state and that a breakout in either direction is possible. The trend may turn bullish or bearish after a pattern breakout. *Figure 11.23* will show you both symmetrical patterns.

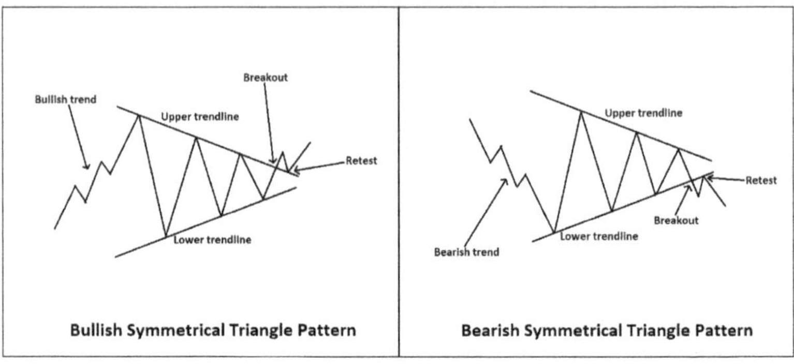

Figure 11.23

Now, I will show you how these patterns look in a real candlestick chart. Figure 11.24 shows the chart of Reliance Inds on a weakly timeframe after an uptrend price consolidated and created a symmetrical triangular formation, when buyers joined the market due to significant purchasing pressure, the market broke the pattern and pushed the price upward.

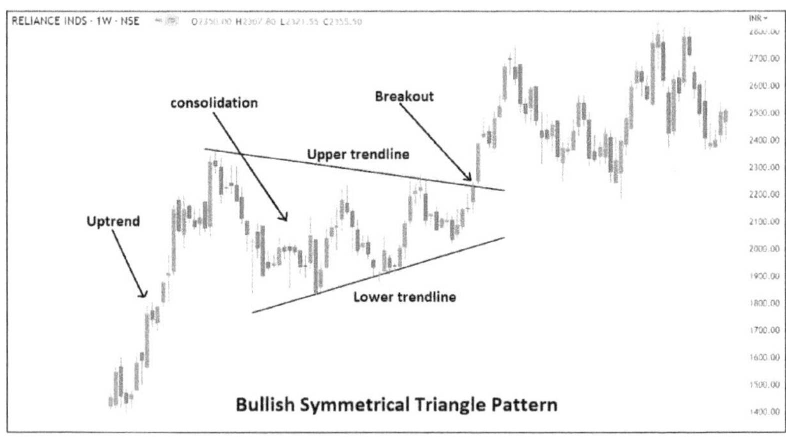

figure 11.24

In figure 11.25, Dr. Reddys Labs chart shown on a 4-hour time frame in which you can see that after a bearish trend, the price consolidated at the movement and made the same pattern as the previous one, but after consolidating, sellers entered the market and the market broke the pattern and pushed the price downward.

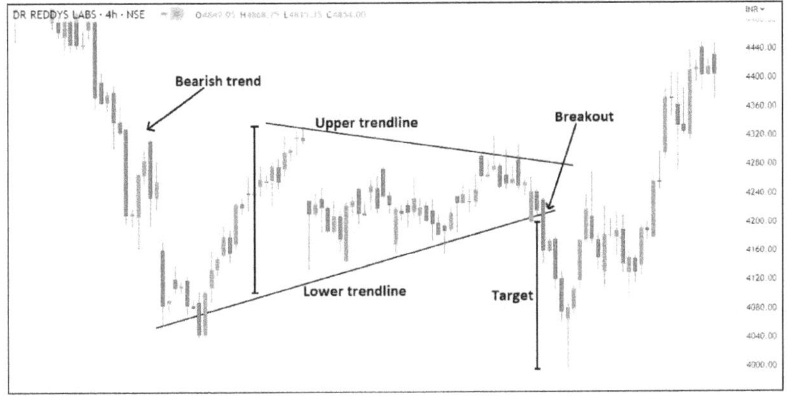

figure 11.25

Now, Some of you may be thinking that, as I stated, there is no trend continuation in this pattern that I have shown you, but if you look at the chart attentively, you will notice that after the breakout, the price hits the target and then returns.

<u>Rising channel Pattern:</u> This pattern is also known as Ascending channel pattern. When the price of an asset is rising within two parallel trendlines that slope upwards. It denotes a phase of consolidation within an uptrend in which the price oscillates between the upper (resistance) and lower trendlines (support) as shown in *figure 11.26*. Breakout is not defined in these types of patterns it can be bullish or bearish.

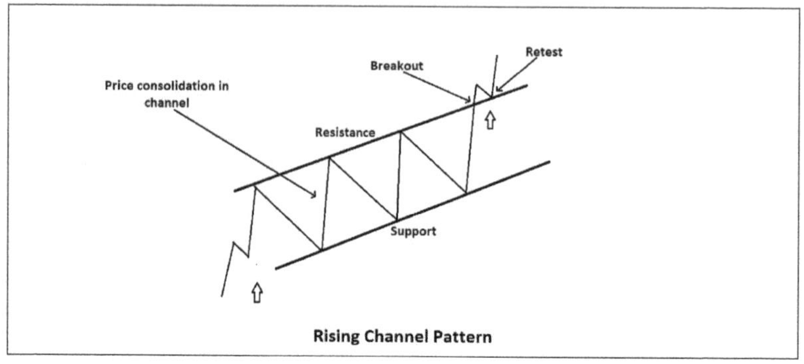

figure 11.26

Now, here some of the characteristics are given of rising channel pattern:-

1. <u>Trendlines:</u> Two parallel trendlines form the pattern, with the higher trendline functioning as resistance and the lower trendline working as support. These trendlines should be designed in such a way that they capture the greatest amount of price touches while forming a well-defined channel.

2. Price movement: Price Movement Within the channel, the price tends to go higher, creating higher highs and lower lows, indicating an uptrend. Typically, the price bounces off the lower trendline (support) and retraces to the upper trendline (resistance).

3. Channel Width: The width of the channel can vary, and wider channels can indicate a stronger trend, while narrower channels can indicate a weaker trend.

4. Breakout Potential: The rising channel pattern indicates that the asset is in an uptrend, with a bullish breakthrough above the upper trendline possible. A breakout happens when the price breaks above the upper trendline with higher volume, signifying the possibility of an uptrend continuation.

A rising channel pattern can be used as a trading signal by traders who start long positions (buying) when the price rebounds off the lower trendline (support) and sell or take profit when the price approaches the higher trendline (resistance). They may also look for a breakout over the upper trendline as proof of the uptrend's likely continuation.

Now, see how this pattern looks in an actual candlestick chart in *figure 11.27*. I utilized a 1-day time frame chart of Tata Steel Limited after an upswing price stabilized and formed a channel pattern after bullish momentum it broke the resistance level and moved upwards.

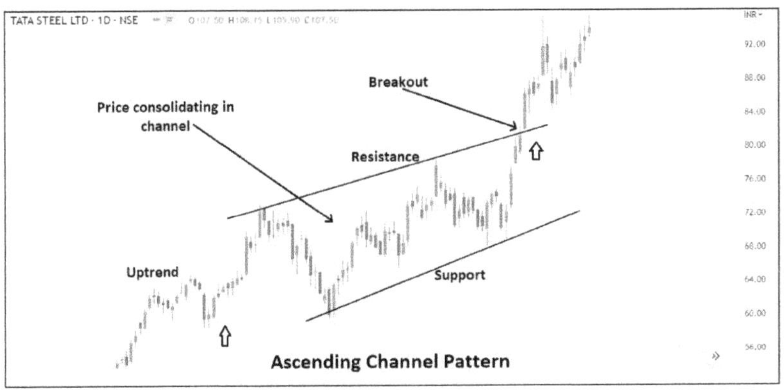

figure 11.27

Falling channel: An asset's price moves between two parallel trendlines that slope downward, forming a channel-like shape. As the price tends to make lower highs and lower lows within the channel, this pattern signals a likely negative trend as shown in *figure 11.28.* It is the inverse of the rising channel and has no breakout certainty for either the upside or the downside; it may be on either side.

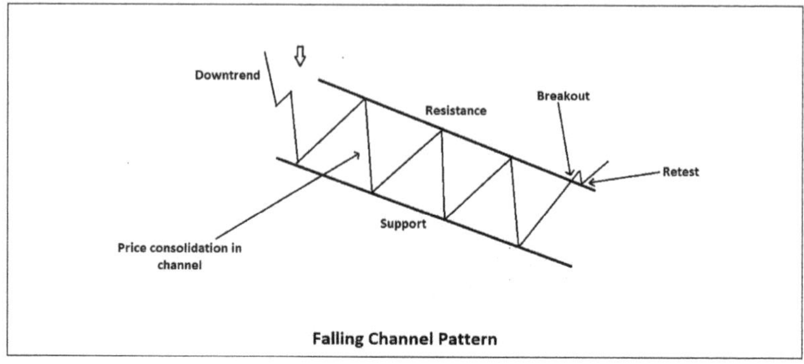

figure 11.28

Some points of this pattern are discussed below:

1. <u>Parallel trendlines:</u> A falling channel pattern is defined by two parallel trendlines, the higher trendline functioning as resistance and the lower trendline as support. These trendlines should be created in such a way that they capture price movement as it moves lower within the channel.

2. <u>The downward slope at starting:</u> A falling channel pattern's upper and lower trendlines should both slope downward, showing a trend of lower highs and lower lows. This means that selling pressure is likely to prevail, and the price may continue to fall.

3. <u>Price oscillation within the channel:</u> The price of the falling channel pattern tends to oscillate between the upper and lower trendlines, with traders looking for prospective trading opportunities based on price activity at these trendlines. Price may encounter resistance at the higher trendline and support at the lower trendline, potentially resulting in trade signals.

4. <u>Breakout Potential:</u> A falling channel pattern may indicate that the price is consolidating within a bearish trend and may potentially break out of the channel in a downward direction.

Traders frequently seek a verified breakout below the lower trendline as a potential signal to begin short positions, since it may indicate that the bearish trend will continue.

In figure 11.29, a 1 day chart of Ultratech cement is shown with a falling channel pattern developed after a selling pressure, as you can see after a selling pressure, the price consolidated in a channel, and when buyers were active, they pushed the price upward.

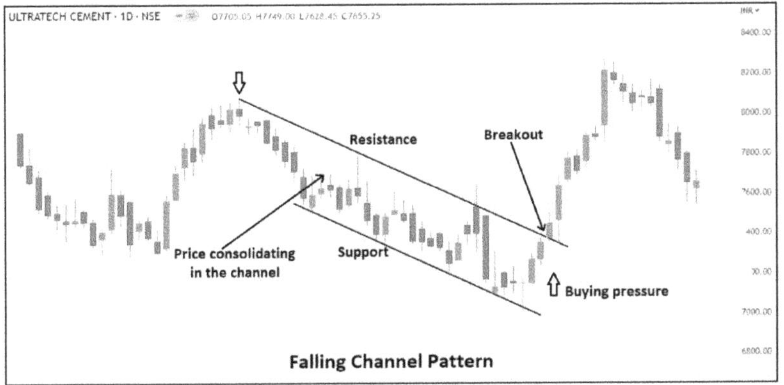

figure 11.29

3. *Continuous chart patterns:*

A continuous chart pattern is one that occurs over time and shows the likely continuance of the current trend. These patterns are produced by the price movements of an item, such as stocks, currency, or commodities, and can provide information about the price's future direction.

Some of the continuous chart patterns are discussed below:

- Bullish Flag
- Bearish Flag

- Bullish Falling Wedge
- Bearish Rising Wedge
- Cup and Handle

Bullish Flag: It is a popular continuation chart pattern that occurs during an upswing and shows the possibility of the positive trend continuing.

It's formed by a brief consolidation or correction following a strong price advance, and it looks like a flagpole and a flag as shown in *figure 11.30*.

The pattern's flag is often a small rectangular-shaped consolidation that slopes against the overall trend, resembling a flag.

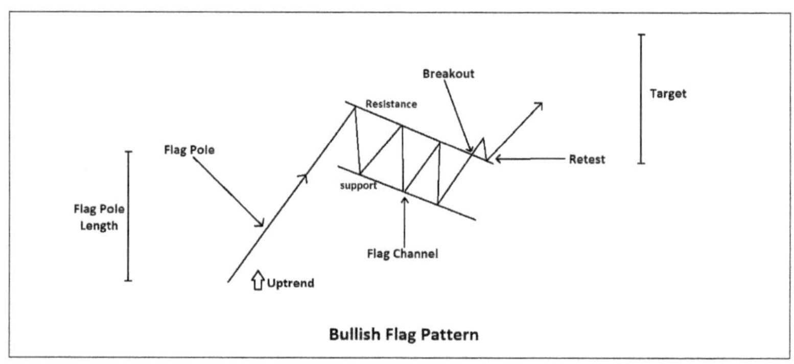

figure 11.30

There are 5 parts of this pattern which is discussed below:

Uptrend: The bullish flag pattern develops within the backdrop of an established uptrend, with a clear and powerful upward price movement.

Flag Pole: The flagpole is the initial strong price movement preceding the flag. It is often a sharp and steep price gain, marking the uptrend's initial impulsive surge.

<u>Flag Channel:</u> The flag is a consolidation phase that comes after the flagpole. It is often a modest rectangular-shaped design that slopes counter-trend. The flag may also experience a minor price decline.

<u>Breakout:</u> The bullish flag pattern is confirmed when the price rises above the flag's top trendline, accompanied by an increase in volume. This is usually interpreted as an indication that the preceding rise will continue.

<u>Price target:</u> The bullish flag pattern's price goal is often computed by measuring the height of the flagpole(approx) and projecting it higher from the breakout point. However, not all flag patterns achieve their price predictions, and other technical analysis tools and market conditions should be evaluated for confirmation.

Now, we will see how it actually looks in a candlestick chart. In figure 11.31 HDFC Life Insurance Chart is shown on a daily timeframe you can see that a flag pattern is formed here after an uptrend. The market consolidated in a flag shape channel and after giving the breakout price hit the target.

figure 11.31

Bearish Flag: The bearish flag pattern is a technical chart pattern that can appear in financial markets during a decline. It is a continuation pattern, indicating that the current decline may continue after a brief respite. It is the opposite of the bullish flag pattern with same characteristics and parts. *Figure 11.32* shows how a bearish flag looks like.

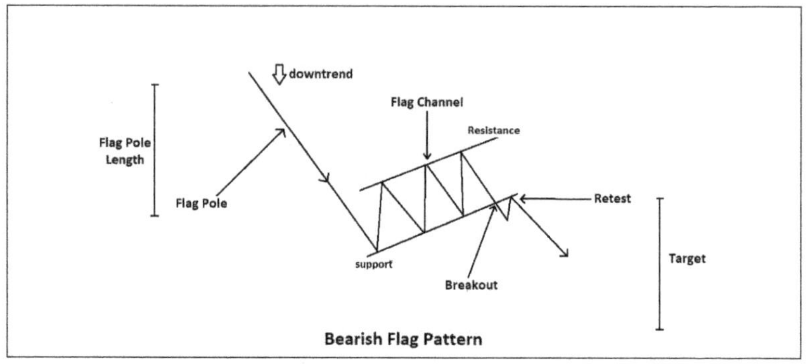

Figure 11.32

There are 4 parts of this pattern after the downtrend which are discussed below:

Flag pole: The flagpole is a sharp and steep downward price movement that signals the first leg of a downtrend. It is typically preceded by a significant bearish price impulse.

Flag: The flag is a minor price consolidation or sideways price range that follows the flagpole. It is typically characterized by lower trading volume and can be viewed as a temporary pause or consolidation period following the initial downtrend.

Breakout: The pattern is completed when the price falls below the flag's lower trendline, indicating a possible continuation of the downtrend.

Price Target: The bearish flag pattern's price objective is calculated by measuring the height of the flagpole (approx) and projecting it downwards from the breakout point. This provides an estimate of the probable downward move.

Now, we will see what it looks like in a real candle stick chart. In *figure 11.33* the graph of Tata Motors LTD has shown on 1-day time frame in which an inverse flag (bearish flag) is formed after downtrend.

figure 11.33

Bullish Falling Wedge: A bullish falling wedge is a technical chart pattern that often indicates a potential bullish price trend reversal.

It is formed by converging trendlines that slant downward, with both the top (resistance) and lower (support) trendlines slanting downward, resulting in a wedge-like shape as shown in *figure 11.34*. Within the falling wedge pattern, the price tends to contract, with lower highs and lower lows indicating a weaker bearish trend.

The bullish falling wedge pattern is considered positive because it indicates that selling pressure is progressively lessening and buyers may be entering the market. As the price reaches the pinnacle of the falling wedge, it shows that the range between resistance and support is closing, potentially indicating an upside breakout.

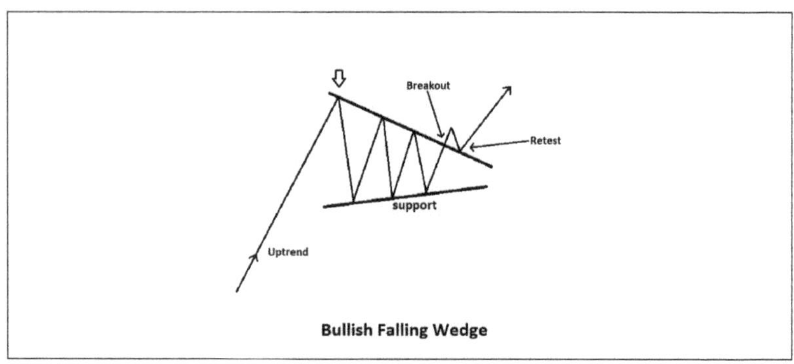

figure 11.34

Figure 11.35 depicts the chart of Oil & Natural Gas in a one-day time frame in which when the price breaks out above the upper trendline of a falling wedge pattern, it is sometimes interpreted as a potentially bullish signal, signaling that the price is prepared for an upward rise.

Figure 11.35

Bearish Rising Wedge: The rising wedge pattern is a technical chart pattern that is usually considered bearish and may indicate a possible price trend reversal. Converging trendlines that slant upward form a wedge-like shape, with the higher trendline (resistance) slanting steeper than the lower trendline (support) as shown in *figure 11.36*.

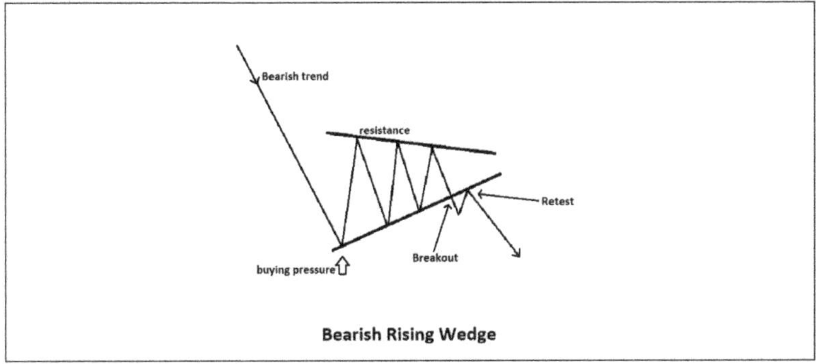

figure 11.36

The rising wedge pattern is distinguished by higher highs and lower lows, but price consolidation is within the narrowing range. This pattern indicates that buying pressure is waning and that sellers may seize control, potentially leading to a bearish breakout.

To trade a bearish rising wedge pattern, traders typically wait for the price to break below the lower boundary of the pattern with high volume and then enter a short position.

On the next page *Figure 11.37* shows you what the bearish rising wedge looks like.

Figure 11.37

Cup and Handle: The cup and handle pattern is a bullish technical chart pattern that is frequently used to indicate probable continuation patterns in price developments. It gets its name from the chart's resemblance to a teacup and handles shape. This pattern can be seen in *figure 11.38.*

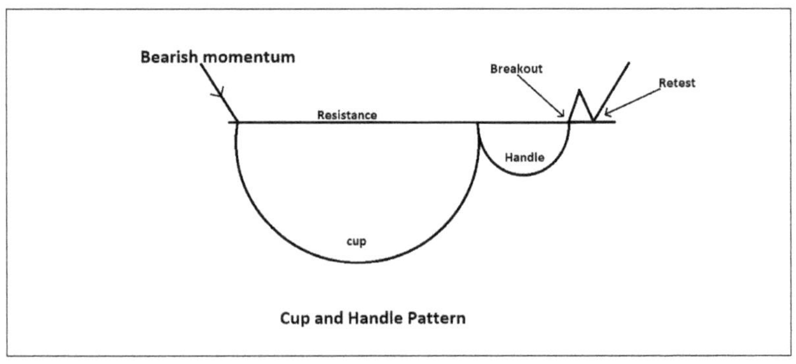

figure 11.38

This pattern looks in candlestick chart as given in *figure 11.39:*

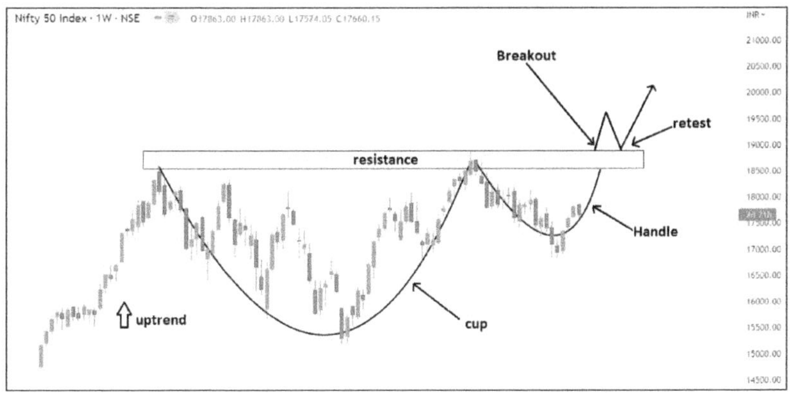

figure 11.39

The cup and handle pattern is formed after a protracted uptrend and is composed of two parts:

- **Cup:** The pattern's initial component is a rounded, U-shaped cup formation that suggests a period of price consolidation or correction. During this stage, the price may pull back and form a cup-shaped rounded bottom.
- **Handle:** The pattern's second component is a smaller consolidation or correction that emerges following the cup development. It usually takes the form of a short downward-sloping trendline known as the handle, which is positioned on the cup's right side.

The cup and handle pattern is considered bullish since it implies that the price will continue to rise following the consolidation period. To validate the probable bullish continuation, traders and investors frequently search for confirmation signals such as higher volume, bullish candlestick patterns, or other technical indicators.

When the price breaks out above the handle trendline, it is often interpreted as a potential bullish indicator, signaling that the price is prepared to move higher.

XII

Indicators

What are Indicators?

Trading indicators identify trading opportunities and prospective market trends based on the analysis and interpretation of price data in order to identify trading opportunities. The price indicators are often derived from mathematical calculations of past price data and are displayed on a trading chart as visual representations of these calculations. One of the key benefits of using indicators in trading is that they can help traders filter out market noise and focus on the most important signals Indicators can assist traders in identifying trends, support and resistance levels, momentum, and prospective trading opportunities by evaluating price and volume data.

Why do we use Indicators?

Traders can use trading indicators for a number of different reasons:

1. **<u>To identify entry and exit points</u>:** The use of indicators can aid traders in spotting potential entry and exit points as well as market buying and selling opportunities.

2. **<u>To identify trends</u>**: There are a variety of indicators available to help traders identify the direction of a market trend, regardless of whether it is up, down, or sideways.

3. **<u>To measure risk</u>**: Bollinger Bands and other volatility indicators, such as those used to gauge risk, can assist traders. When deciding on stop loss levels and other risk management techniques, this can be especially helpful.

4. **<u>To confirm price action</u>**: Indicators can be utilized to support or undermine what the price action is indicating. For instance, a negative divergence between price and momentum indicators may indicate that the upward trend is waning and may be about to reverse.

5. **<u>To provide objective data</u>**: Indicators give traders access to objective data that can aid in their decision-making. Traders can lessen the influence of emotions and biases in their trading decisions by employing indicators to assess market data.

Therefore, Indicators are generally used in trading to assist traders in spotting prospective trading opportunities, calculating risk, and making better trading decisions. Indicators should always be used in conjunction with other methods of analysis and risk management techniques because they are not perfect.

Types of Indicators:

There are many different kinds of indicators used in trading; a few of the most popular ones are listed below:

- Trend Indicators
- Momentum Indicators
- Volatility Indicators
- Volume Indicators
- Support & Resistance Indicators

1. *Trend Indicators*

The techniques used in trading to determine the market trend's direction are known as trend indicators. They are intended to minimize price swings and emphasize the general trend. The theory behind trend indicators is that by spotting the trend, traders may make better trading selections because prices have a tendency to move in a particular direction over time. There are several types of trend indicators, including moving averages and the Average Directional Index (ADX). From them moving averages is more popular among traders, ninety percent of traders use this indicator in their trading strategy. Let us discuss them one by one.

Moving Averages: Moving averages are a common technical analysis method in trading that is used to smooth out price swings and determine the underlying trend. They function by computing the average price of an asset over a given time period and plotting it on a chart.

Moving averages are important for recognizing patterns since they provide a visual depiction of the average price over time. Traders can assess if the current price is above or below the moving average by comparing it to the average, indicating a bullish or bearish trend.

Moving averages are classified into two types: simple moving averages (SMA) and exponential moving averages (EMA). The SMA determines the average price over a given number of time periods, whereas the EMA emphasizes recent values.

Traders often use moving averages to identify support and resistance levels, which can be used as entry and exit points for trades.

For example, see *figure 12.1* chart of Reliance Inds is shown on 1-day time frame, I have used the moving average exponential, if the price of an asset is trending above the moving average, traders may look for buying opportunities when the price dips below the moving average and then bounces back up. Conversely, if the price is trending below the moving average, traders may look for selling opportunities when the price rises above the moving average and then drops back down.

figure 12.1

<u>Average Directional Index (ADX)</u>: In a financial market, this indicator is used to assess the strength of a trend. The ADX is commonly used to determine if a market is trending or not, as well as the strength of the trend. The directional movement indicators (+DI and -DI), which quantify the strength of upward and downward moves in a market over a predetermined time period, are used to construct the ADX.

The absolute value of the difference between the two directional movement indicators is then multiplied by the sum of the two indicators to determine the ADX.

A weak trend is indicated by a value of 20 or lower, approx 30 is medium and a strong trend is indicated by a value of 40 or higher for the ADX, which normally varies between 0 and 100. Like in *figure 12.2* graph of Nifty 50 is shown in which the value of ADX of the marked points is more than 40 that means its a strong bearish trend.

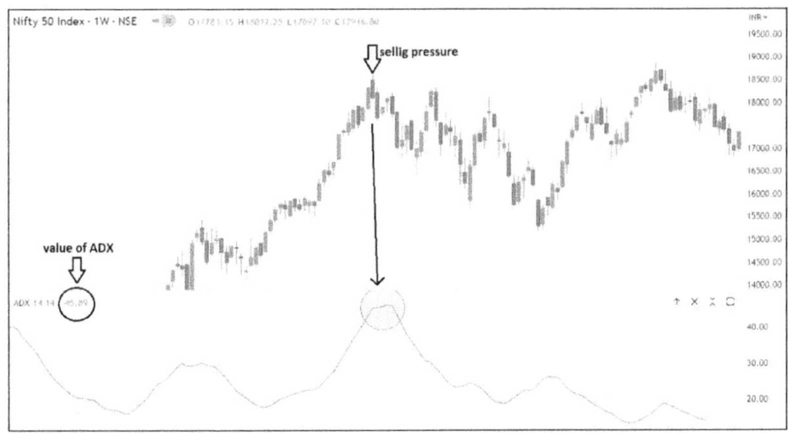

figure 12.2

The ADX can be used by traders to determine whether a trend is gaining or losing steam, as well as to support probable trend reversals. It's vital to remember that the ADX is not a directional indicator, which means it doesn't reveal the trend's direction. Instead, it assesses how strongly the trend is moving, whether it is upward or downward.

2. *Momentum Indicators*

Indicators that indicate the rate of change in the price of an asset over a given time period. They are used to determine the strength or weakness of a trend as well as to indicate probable reversal points. There are several momentum indicators like Relative Strength Index (RSI), Moving Average Convergence Divergence (MACD). Now we will discuss them one by one .

<u>Relative Strength Index (RSI)</u>: To measure the strength and momentum of a financial asset's price movement, traders frequently use the Relative Strength Index (RSI), a prominent technical indicator. The idea of momentum, on which the RSI is built, contends that price moves often persist in the same direction until a material reversal takes place.

The RSI is calculated using the average gain and loss of an asset's price over a given period of time. The formula for calculating the RSI is: _RSI = 100 - [100 / (1 + RS)]_

RS (Relative Strength) is determined by dividing the asset's average gain over a certain period by its average loss over the same time period. The RSI normally has a range of 0 to 100, with values above 70 signifying that an asset is overbought and may be due for a price correction and below 30 signifying that an asset is oversold and may be due for a price rebound. The RSI is widely used with other technical indicators by traders to help them discover potential buy and sell signals. For instance, if an asset's RSI is above 70, it may be a sign that the asset is overbought and that traders should think about selling.

On the other hand, if an asset's RSI is below 30, it can be a sign that it is oversold, and traders might think about purchasing. Like take an example of _figure 12.3_ in which chart of Hindustan Uniliver chart is shown on 1 weak time frame you can see on the marked point the value of RSI is more than 70 which is clear sign of selling similarly if that value is below 30 we can go with buying.

figure 12.3

<u>Moving Average Convergence Divergence (MACD)</u>: It is a well-liked technical indicator that's employed in trading to spot potential trend reversals and changes in the momentum of financial assets. The 26-day exponential moving average (EMA) is subtracted from the 12-day EMA to calculate the MACD.

Two lines make up the MACD indicator: the MACD line, which represents the difference between the two EMAs, and the signal line, which is an extension of the MACD line by nine days. In order to give traders a visual depiction of the strength and direction of the price momentum of a financial asset, the MACD line oscillates above and below the signal line.

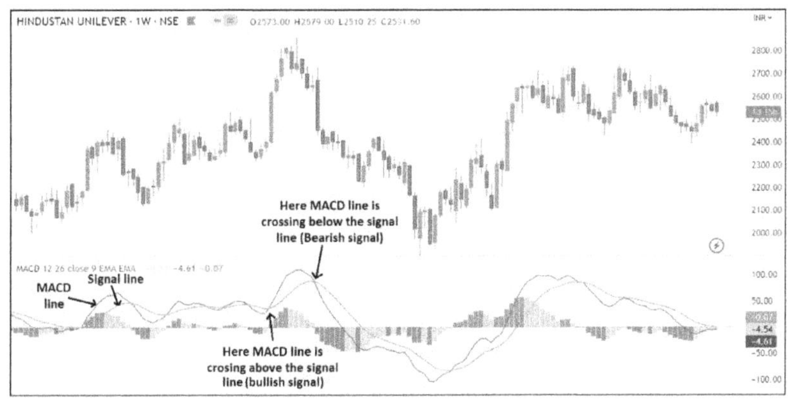

figure 12.4

A bullish signal is one that suggests that the price of the asset may be going to increase when the MACD line crosses above the signal line. On the other hand, it is typically regarded as a negative signal when the MACD line crosses below the signal line, implying that the asset's price may be poised to decline as shown in *figure 12.4*. The separation between the MACD line and the signal line is another factor that traders consider. A stronger trend is shown by a bigger gap between the two lines, while a weaker trend is indicated by a smaller gap.

3. Volatility Indicators:

A technical indicator called a volatility indicator is one that's used in trading to gauge how volatile a financial asset's price movements are. Because they can help traders understand the possible risk and return of a trade, volatility indicators are crucial. The Bollinger Bands and Average True Range (ATR) are the examples of volatility indicators.

Bollinger Bands: A common technical indicator used in trading to assess the volatility of a financial asset is Bollinger Bands. The indicator comprises of two bands that are drawn above and below the moving average, as well as a moving average (usually a 20-period simple moving average). The bands' width depends on how volatile the asset is; broader bands denote higher volatility, while narrower bands denote lesser volatility as shown in *figure 12.5.*

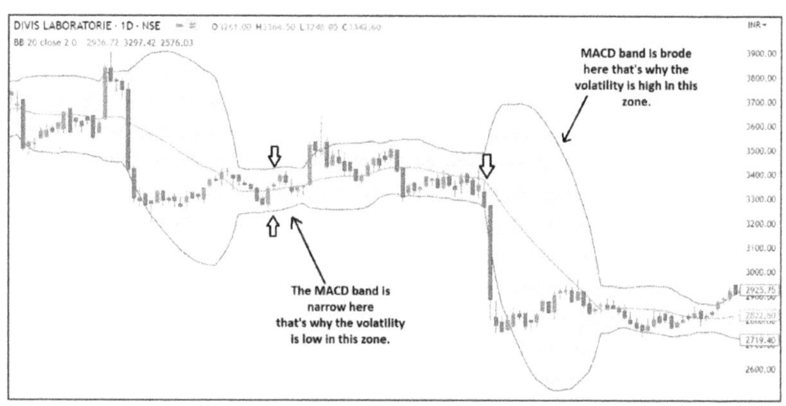

figure 12.5

Based on the asset's current volatility, traders can also utilize Bollinger Bands to pinpoint future price goals and stop-loss levels. For instance, using a tighter stop-loss level may be more appropriate if the bands are relatively narrow, whereas larger bands may signal the need for a wider stop-loss level to account for more possible volatility.

<u>Average True Range (ATR)</u>: A technical indicator called the Average True Range (ATR) is used to gauge the volatility of a financial asset. J. Welles Wilder created it, and traders use it frequently to set stop-loss levels and choose the right position size for a transaction.

The average of a number of true range values over a predetermined amount of time is used to calculate the ATR. The difference between the current high and the previous close, the difference between the current low and the current close, and the difference between the current high and the current low are used to determine the real range.

The ATR's calculated value is expressed in the same money or pip units as the asset's price. More volatility is indicated by a larger ATR value, while lesser volatility is indicated by a lower value as shown in the *figure 12.6* in which value of ATR can be seen marked, where the market is volatile and where not.

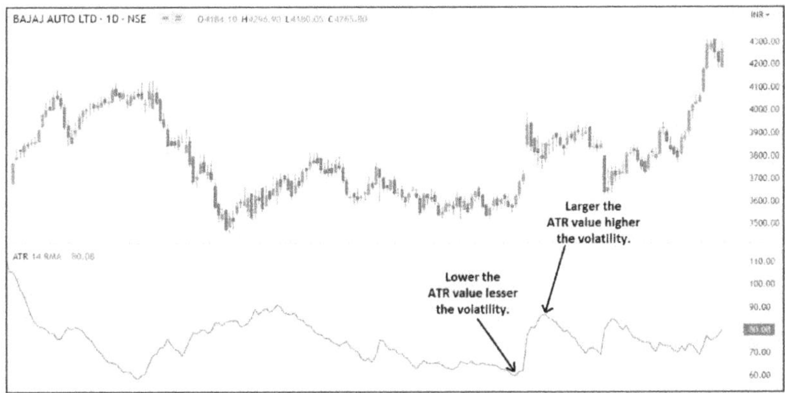

figure 12.6

By multiplying the ATR value by a specific multiple (such 2 or 3), deducting or adding that sum from the entry price for a long position or adding it to the entry price for a short position, traders can utilize the ATR to create stop-loss levels. This enables traders to set stop-loss levels while taking into consideration the asset's current volatility.

4. Volume Indicator:

volume Indicator: A technical analysis tool called the volume indicator counts the shares, contracts, or lots of a financial instrument that have been exchanged during a specific period of time.

Traders frequently use it to validate price trends and spot potential changes in the trend's direction.

The volume indicator is often shown underneath a financial asset's price chart as a histogram or a line graph.

The amount of trading activity during the relevant time period is shown by the height of the bars in the histogram or the value of the line graph. Greater volume typically denotes more intense market buying or selling pressure.

By checking for rising or falling volume levels that match the trend's direction, traders can use the volume indicator to validate a price trend.

For instance, rising prices and increased volume may indicate that the market is experiencing significant bullish momentum.

On the other hand, if prices are declining and volume is rising, it may indicate that the market is experiencing a significant bearish momentum as shown in *figure 12.7* on the next page.

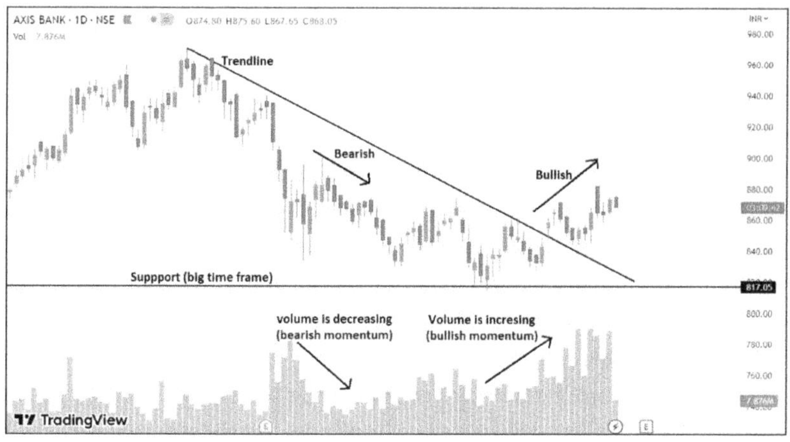

figure 12.7

The volume indicator can be used to spot probable changes in a trend's trajectory. A reversal may be on the horizon, for instance, if prices are rising but volume is declining. This would indicate that the bullish momentum is waning. In a similar vein, falling prices with declining volume could indicate that the bearish momentum is waning and that a reversal may be on the horizon as shown in *figure 12.7. The table* below will summarize the above.

PRICE	VOLUME	RESULT
UP	UP	STRONG BULLISH MOMENTUM
UP	DOWN	BULLISH MOMENTUM
DOWN	UP	STRONG BEARISH MOMENTUM
DOWN	DOWN	BEARISH MOMENTUM

5. *Support & Resistance Indicators:*

Traders can locate possible market support and resistance levels by using a support and resistance indicator. Moving averages and Fibonacci retracements are examples of the numerous sorts of indicators that can be employed for this. from these moving averages we have already discussed in trend indicators now let's discuss Fibonacci retracements.

Fibonacci retracements:

To locate probable levels of support and resistance in the market, traders frequently employ the Fibonacci retracements technical analysis tool. These levels can help traders manage risk more skillfully and make better trading decisions.

To determine probable levels of market support and resistance. The idea is based on the mathematical Fibonacci sequence, where each number is the product of its two preceding numbers (e.g., 0, 1, 1, 2, 3, 5, 8, 13, 21, 34, 55, etc.). This pattern is common in nature and has also been observed in financial markets.

Traders must first detect a big price movement in the market, such as a significant uptrend or downtrend, before employing Fibonacci retracements. Then they mark the retracement levels—possible points where the price can run into support or resistance—with lines on the chart.

Based on the Fibonacci ratios of 23.6%, 38.2%, 50%, 61.8%, and 100%, the retracement levels are calculated. These levels show how much of the price move has been retraced; the shallowest retracement level is 23.6%, and the deepest retracement level is 61.8%.

The retracement threshold would be 50%, For example, *figure 12.8* shows the chart of IndusInd bank on a weak timeframe simply use the Fibonacci retracement by marking the low price level to the high price level as shown in the figure. Here, the stock price increased from ?759 to ?1270 before falling down to ?1014.

Depending on the trend, traders may utilize the 50% retracement level as a potential level of support or resistance as in the figure bullish trend is going on so that level will act as a support level.

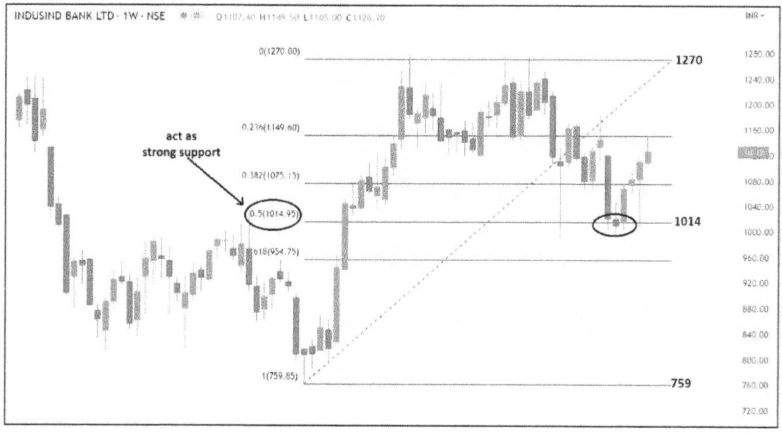

figure 12.8

In order to provide a more thorough study of the market, Fibonacci retracements are frequently utilized in conjunction with other technical analysis tools like trend lines and moving averages. Fibonacci retracements can also be used by traders to set stop-loss orders and identify potential entry and exit locations for trades.

XIII
Stoploss

What is Stoploss?

A stop-loss is a tool used in trading to limit potential losses on a transaction. It is an order made with a broker to sell a security when it reaches a predetermined price, known as the stop price.

The idea of a stop-loss is to limit how much money an investor can lose on a trade. A stop-loss order instructs the broker to sell the security if the price falls below a certain level. This can be utilized to reduce the risk of staying in a position that is losing value.

For example, if trading equities, foreign exchange, or futures contracts, stop-loss orders can be employed in various trading circumstances. They are especially helpful in volatile markets where losses can increase quickly and prices change drastically.

For example see *Figure 13.1*, if an investor buys shares of stock at 80 rupees each and places a stop-loss order at 70 rupees, the broker will immediately sell the stock if it drops to 70 rupees or less. Instead of enabling them to keep holding the stock as it might lose more value, this would cap the investor's losses at rupees 10 per share.

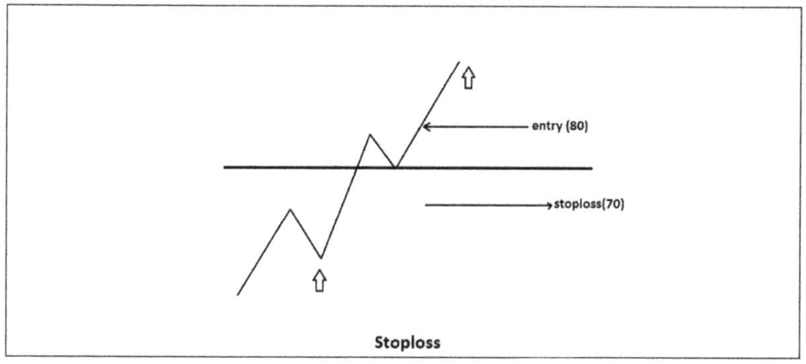

figure 13.1

It's important to keep in mind that stop-loss orders are not failsafe, though. They might occasionally fail to execute at the predetermined price as a result of slippage or market gaps. A stop-loss that is too close to the present price can also cause the order to be executed too quickly before the security has had a chance to rebound.

Why Stoploss is Essential?

Stop-loss orders are important in trading since they help to manage risk and protect capital. When an investor enters a trade, they expose themselves to potential losses if the trade fails. A stop-loss order specifies an exit point, limiting the amount of money that an investor might potentially lose on a trade.

Without a stop-loss, an investor may continue to maintain a losing position in the hope that the market will eventually turn in their favor. But, if the market continues to go against them, this strategy might result in huge losses. An investor can limit their potential losses and terminate the trade once the price hits a specified level by placing a stop-loss order.

Stop-loss orders are especially useful in volatile markets where prices can change quickly. A position in these markets can quickly shift against an investor, resulting in large losses. Investors can protect themselves from the possible downside of these unpredictable fluctuations by utilizing a stop-loss order.

Another reason why stop-loss orders are so important is that they help to eliminate emotions from trading decisions. Fear and greed, for example, can often distort an investor's judgment and lead to illogical decision-making. Setting a stop-loss allows investors to trade more rationally and limit their potential losses based on a specified departure point.

Types of Stoploss?

Traders can utilise a variety of stop-loss orders in their trading. Each sort of stop-loss order serves a distinct purpose, and traders should carefully assess which type is most suited to their trading strategy. Now we'll go over each one individually.

1. Fixed Stoploss
2. Trailing Stoploss
3. Volatility Stoploss
4. Time Stoploss
5. Margin Stoploss

1. Fixed Stoploss

In trading, a fixed stop-loss order defines a predetermined price level at which the trader will close out a position if the price swings against them. The most popular and simple way to manage risk in trading is using a stop-loss order of this kind.

A trader who uses a fixed stop-loss order selects a predetermined price at which they are prepared to sell their asset in order to reduce possible losses. A trader might establish a fixed stop-loss at 90 rupees , for instance, if they purchase a stock at 100 rupees. The stop-loss order is activated and the trader's position is automatically closed if the stock price drops to 90 rupees as shown in *figure 13.2.*

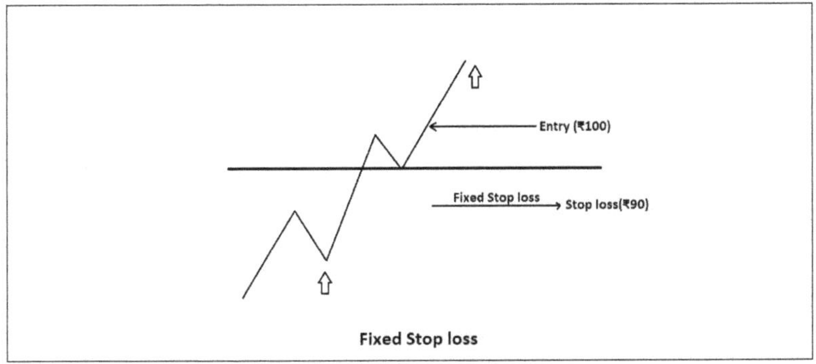

figure 13.2

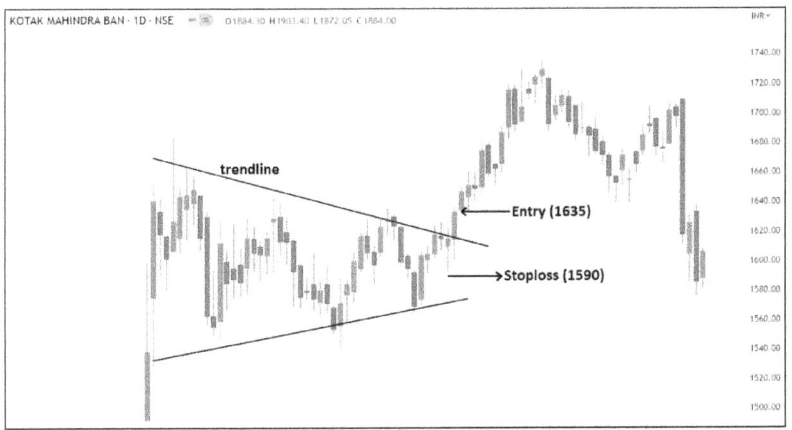

Figure 13.3

Figure 13.3 now demonstrates where to put this stop loss into a genuine candlestick chart. I've included a daily timeframe chart of

Kotak Mahindra Bank so you can see the candles clearly making a bullish patent pattern after consolidating it delivered a breakout. We can enter at ?1635 and set a stop loss at ?1590; the difference between these two prices represents our risk, which is ?45.

Fixed stop-loss orders give traders a clear exit strategy in the event that the market moves against them, making them a useful risk management tool. Traders can reduce their potential losses and safeguard their funds by setting a defined stop-loss.

Advantage: A fixed stop-loss order's ease of use and comprehension is one of its key features. To choose the right level for the stop-loss order, traders might utilize technical analysis or other market indicators. Unless the trader chooses to change the stop-loss level, the stop-loss does not need to be adjusted after it is set.

Disadvantage: A set stop-loss order has the drawback of not accounting for market volatility or price changes. Even if the asset is expected to rebound in the future, a fixed stop-loss order may be activated in an extremely turbulent market. If traders close a position too soon, they risk losing out on possible gains.

However, a predetermined stop-loss is a useful tool for trading risk management. It enables traders to protect their capital and reduce their possible losses. Trading strategies, market conditions, and volatility should all be taken into account when determining the right level for a set stop-loss order.

2. *Trailing Stoploss:*

A dynamic stop-loss order used in trading is called a trailing stop-loss. It is made to move with the price of an asset as it changes in the trader's favor. By establishing a stop-loss level that changes in step with the price swings of the asset, it enables traders to safeguard their gains and reduce prospective losses.

With a trailing stop-loss order, a trader specifies a level in percentage or money below the current market price at which the position will be closed in the event of a price decline. The stop-loss level rises together with the asset's price as it rises, keeping a specified distance from the current market price.

For instance, the initial stop-loss level would be rupees 45, if a trader purchases a stock at 50 rupees and sets a trailing stop-loss of 10% below the current market price as shown in *figure 13.4*.

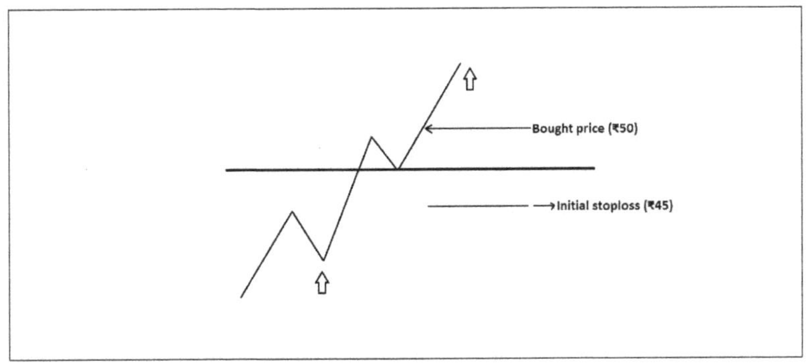

figure 13.4

The stop-loss level would increase to 54 rupees if the stock price increased to rupees 60 as shown in *figure 13.5*. The Trade would be automatically closed if the stock fell to 54 rupees or less.

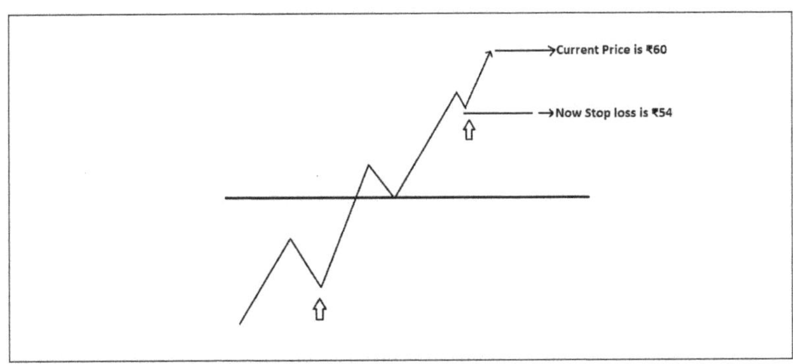

figure 13.5

Traders who want to safeguard their gains and curtail their potential losses can benefit from using trailing stop-loss orders. Following the asset's price changes allows traders to lock in profits if it swings in their favour while still allowing the item to rise in value.

Advantage: The ability to profit from the momentum of an asset's price movement is one advantage of trailing stop-loss orders. The stop-loss level will raise along with the asset price if it keeps rising, enabling traders to make more money. When an asset's price is going strong in one direction in a trending market, trailing stop-loss orders are very useful.

Disadvantage: The fact that trailing stop-loss orders can be vulnerable to market noise and volatility. However, one of its drawbacks. Wide price swings for the asset may cause the stop-loss level to be activated early, resulting in lost opportunities or unneeded losses.

To summarise, a trailing stop-loss order is a dynamic risk management strategy that allows traders to track the price swings of an asset while protecting their profits. Traders should carefully assess the optimal level for their trailing stop-loss order, taking market conditions, volatility, and trading technique into account.

3. Volatility Stoploss:

A volatility stop-loss is a form of stop-loss order used in trading that adjusts the stop-loss level based on the degree of market volatility. To reduce possible losses and safeguard gains, it is built to dynamically alter the stop-loss level based on the amount of market volatility.

Volatility stop-loss orders calculate the ideal level for the stop-loss order using a measure of volatility, such as the Average True Range (ATR). The average price range for a certain time period is measured by the ATR, a technical indicator. More volatility is indicated by a larger ATR, while decreased volatility is indicated by a lower ATR.

An ATR-based distance or percentage below the current market price is specified when a trader places a volatility stop-loss order. A trader might, for instance, establish a volatility stop-loss two times the ATR below the price of the current market. Take, for instance, figure 13.6, which displays a chart of ITC LTD over a significant amount of time. If we enter at 235 rupees in that case, then our stop loss is 30 rupees (which is double than ATR value) below the price we enter.

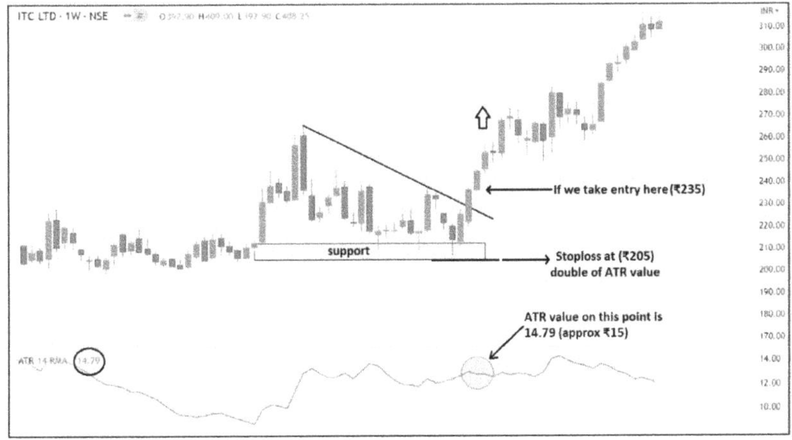

figure 13.6

Advantage: The benefit of utilizing a volatility stop-loss order is that it modifies the stop-loss level in accordance with the degree of market volatility. The stop-loss level would be set further from the present market price in extremely volatile markets to take into consideration the higher risk of significant price swings. The stop-loss level would be positioned nearer to the current market price in low-volatility markets, lowering the risk of losses.

Disadvantage: The complexity of calculating and implementing a volatility stop-loss order is one drawback. To choose the ideal level for the stop-loss order, traders must have a solid grasp of technical analysis and the ATR indicator.

In summary, a volatility stop-loss order modifies the stop-loss level dependent on the degree of market volatility. It is a dynamic tool for risk management in trading. Trading strategies, market conditions, and volatility should all be taken into consideration when determining the right level for a volatility stop-loss order. To safeguard their cash and reduce potential losses, it is crucial to utilize this kind of stop-loss in conjunction with other risk management instruments.

4. *Time Stoploss:*

A stop-loss order is known as a "time stop-loss" is one that is based on how much time has passed since a position was opened. It is intended to automatically close the position after a predetermined period of time, independent of the current market price.

A trader establishes a precise time restriction for how long they are willing to keep the position when they place a time stop-loss order. For a certain trade, a trader might, as an example, set a temporal stop-loss of one week. The position will be automatically canceled if the transaction has not generated the required level of profit or has suffered large losses within a week.

Advantage: Using a time stop-loss order has the advantage of preventing traders from holding losing positions for too long, which could result in substantial losses. Also, it can aid traders in resisting the urge to cling to a profitable position for an excessive amount of time at the risk of a market reversal and ensuing loss.

Disadvantage: Yet, if the market continues to move in the trader's favor, utilizing a time stop-loss order may limit the potential for earnings. A trader who places a time stop-loss order too soon risked missing out on potential gains if the market moved in their favor after they closed the position.

After carefully weighing market circumstances, volatility, and trading technique, traders should decide on the right time limit for their time stop-loss order. To increase their potential profits and reduce their possible losses, they can also think about combining time stop-loss orders with additional risk management strategies like trailing stop-loss orders or position sizing.

In conclusion, a time stop-loss order is a risk management strategy used in trading that instantly terminates a position after a predetermined period of time. To safeguard their funds and increase their potential gains, traders can combine time stop-loss orders with other risk management instruments.

5. Margin Stoploss:

A stop-loss order known as a "margin stop-loss" is one that is used in trading and is based on the margin requirements established by the broker. It is intended to automatically close a transaction if the margin requirements are not satisfied, shielding the trader from huge losses and possible margin calls.

A margin stop-loss order specifies a certain margin threshold below which the trader is willing to close the transaction. For one particular deal, a trader might specify a margin stop-loss of 20%. The position will be automatically closed if the margin level drops below 20%.

Advantage: A margin stop-loss order assists traders in managing their margin requirements and avoiding potential margin calls, which can occur when a trader's account does not have enough equity to cover the required margin for their open positions. Margin calls can compel holdings to be liquidated, resulting in severe losses.

Disadvantage: Because market volatility and other factors that can affect a position's performance are not taken into account, utilizing a margin stop-loss order may not be the best risk management strategy for many traders.

Taking into account their broker's margin restrictions, the market's volatility, and their trading technique, traders should carefully determine the right margin level for their margin stop-loss order. To increase their potential profits and reduce their possible losses, they can also think about combining margin stop-loss orders with additional risk management strategies like trailing stop-loss orders or position size.

A margin stop-loss order, which automatically terminates a position if the margin requirements set by the broker are not reached, is a risk management instrument used in trading. Margin stop-loss orders should be used in conjunction with other risk management tools by traders to safeguard their cash and increase possible earnings. In order to guarantee that margin requirements are being satisfied and to prevent potential margin calls, it is crucial to routinely monitor the margin levels of open positions.

How to determine the optimal Stoploss for a particular trade?

It can be difficult to balance the risk of potential losses with the possibility of earnings when determining the best stop-loss level for a given trade. The following actions can be taken by traders to choose the best stop-loss level for a trade:

Evaluate market volatility: Examining the market volatility of the traded asset is one method for figuring out the ideal stop-loss level. To determine the possible range of price changes, traders might utilize technical indicators like average true range (ATR) or standard deviation. Traders might select a stop-loss level that is above the projected range of price changes based on this study.

Consider Support and Resistance level: A different strategy is to take into account the levels of support and resistance. To protect themselves from potential losses in the event that the price breaches these levels, traders can place a stop-loss level below a support level or above a resistance level.

Utilise risk management tools: Traders can also utilize risk management techniques to choose the best stop-loss level, such as position sizing. Traders can set a stop-loss level that restricts their potential losses to a manageable level by assessing the greatest amount of risk they are ready to take on a trade.

Think about this trading technique: The ideal stop-loss level might also be influenced by the trading technique being employed.

For instance, a trend-following strategy would need a looser stop-loss level to account for longer-term price changes, whilst a scalping strategy might need a tighter stop-loss level to prevent potential losses.

Practice with demo account: Demo accounts can be used to practice setting stop-loss settings and evaluating their efficacy by traders. Trading strategies' ideal stop-loss levels can be found by traders who backtest transactions using historical data.

How to use Stoploss in different scenarios?

Depending on the trading circumstance and the trader's risk management plan, stop-loss orders may be used differently. The following are some instances of stop-loss orders being used in various trading scenarios:

Breakout Trading: A trader may employ a volatility stop-loss order based on the asset's range during the consolidation period prior to the breakout. To reduce possible losses if the breakout fails, the stop-loss level may be placed at a particular percentage or dollar amount below the breakout point. A trailing stop-loss order may also be used by the trader to collect profits as the market turns in its favor.

Trend Trading: A trader may employ a predetermined stop-loss order based on market volatility or the average true range (ATR) of the asset being traded in a trend trading strategy. Depending on the trader's risk tolerance, the stop-loss level may be set at a particular percentage or dollar amount below the entry price. A trailing stop-loss order may also be used by the trader to collect profits as the market turns in its favor.

Scalping: If the market goes against a trader's position, they may employ a tight set stop-loss order to reduce potential losses. Depending on the trader's risk tolerance, the stop-loss level may be set at a particular percentage or dollar amount below the entry price. A trailing stop-loss order may also be used by the trader to collect profits as the market turns in its favor.

News Trading: If the market does not move in the trader's favor within a predetermined timeframe following a news announcement, the trader may utilize a time stop-loss order to limit prospective losses. A volatility stop-loss order may also be used by the trader to reduce potential losses in the event that unexpected news causes the market to move against its position.

Common mistakes using Stoploss

Stop-loss orders are a useful risk management technique that can assist traders in limiting possible losses and safeguarding their capital. Yet, they can also be abused, resulting in typical errors that might harm trading performance. When utilizing stop-loss orders, be sure to avoid the following common mistakes:

Too tight of a stop-loss order: Stop-loss orders that are placed too close to the entry price increase the chance of getting stopped out by typical market volatility, which can result in lost profit chances. To ensure that stop-loss orders offer sufficient protection while allowing for potential profits, traders should base them on market volatility and the asset being traded.

Using stop-loss orders as a safe exit: Stop-loss orders have the potential to reduce possible losses, but they do not ensure a certain exit price. Fast-moving markets make it possible for stop-loss orders to be activated at a price that is vastly different from the anticipated exit price, resulting in unforeseen losses. Stop-loss orders should be used in conjunction with other risk management techniques and tools by traders to safeguard their capital.

Not adjusting Stop loss order: Stop-loss orders should be adjusted whenever market conditions change; failing to do so could result in large losses. The stop-loss orders on open positions should be constantly reviewed by traders in light of shifting market conditions.

Not considering news events: News events have a big impact on market volatility, therefore not taking them into account when placing stop-loss orders might result in unforeseen losses. To reduce possible losses, traders should be aware of impending news events and modify their stop-loss orders accordingly.

Too far away stop-loss orders: If the market goes against the trader's position, placing stop-loss orders far from the entry price might result in significant potential losses. When creating stop-loss orders, traders should take into account the likely range of price movements and the item being traded to make sure that they offer sufficient protection without unduly restricting potential profits.

XIV

Risk Management

Define Risk Management ?

Trading risk management entails the process of identifying, evaluating, and minimizing risks that may have an impact on a trading portfolio's profitability.

Trading risk management is developing techniques and instruments to minimize potential losses while optimizing potential rewards. Risk management tactics used by traders include diversification, hedging, and the use of stop-loss orders.

Setting risk management goals and determining acceptable levels of risk are also part of risk management. Traders must assess their risk tolerance and devise risk management methods depending on their objectives and risk tolerance levels.

Effective risk management in trading also requires monitoring and updating risk management measures in response to changing market conditions. The goal of risk management is to minimize the likelihood of losses and protect the trader's capital.

Overall, risk management is essential for traders to maintain wealth and achieve long-term market success. A well-developed risk management plan is essential for managing trading risks and ensuring a trader's long-term ability to trade.

How to identify risk in trading?

A crucial aspect of risk management in trading is risk identification. The following techniques can be used by traders to spot potential dangers in their trading activities:

Examine historical trading data: By examining historical trading data, traders can spot patterns and trends that may point to possible hazards and guide their risk-management plans.

Analyse the market in-depth: Traders can examine market conditions and trends to spot potential hazards related to volatility, liquidity, and other elements that could affect their trading strategy.

Perform a risk assessment: Traders can perform a risk assessment to pinpoint potential risks, assess their likelihood, and consider how they might affect their trading operations.

Types of Risks

Trading involves various types of risks such as market risk, credit risk, operational risk, and liquidity risk, among others. We will discuss them one by one.

Market risk: Market risk is a kind of risk that traders incur as a result of market changes that might impact the value of their investments. Market risk can be caused by various variables, including economic conditions, political events, natural disasters, and interest rate changes, among others. Market risk is one of the most critical hazards that traders must consider when trading.

For example, Assume a trader invests in the equity of a company that operates in the energy sector. A quick decline in oil prices owing to changes in global supply and demand may cause the stock price to collapse, resulting in trading losses. This is an example of market risk, in which external market conditions can have an impact on the value of the trader's investment.

Credit risk:A sort of risk that traders may encounter is credit risk, which arises from the potential for a counterparty to breach a financial obligation. When a trader enters into a transaction with a counterparty, such as a broker or a financial institution, that is unable to uphold its financial commitments, credit risk may occur in the trading environment.

For example, Consider a scenario where a trader purchases a bond issued by a business that subsequently can't make its payments. Credit risk results from the potential for losses for the trader as a result of the default. Alternatively, a trader may encounter credit risk when dealing in derivatives like futures or options if the counterparty breaches the terms of the contract.

<u>Operational risk:</u>Operational risk is a form of risk that traders confront because of the chance of losses caused by insufficient or failing internal processes, systems, or human errors. In trading, operational risk can originate from various sources, including technology breakdowns, fraud, regulatory noncompliance, and transaction processing errors.

Assume a trader places a trade on a trading platform, but the platform experiences a technical issue, causing the trade to fail and the trader to lose money. This is an example of operational risk, in which an internal process or system fails, resulting in financial loss.

Another kind of operational risk is when a trader performs a trade based on inaccurate market information as a result of a human mistake. For example, a trader may enter an inaccurate price for a deal, resulting in a loss as a result of incorrect information.

<u>Liquidity risk:</u>Liquidity risk is a form of risk that traders experience because they may not be able to sell an item quickly enough to avoid a loss or meet financial obligations. Liquidity risk in trading can emerge from various variables, including market circumstances, trade volume, and the availability of buyers and sellers.

For example, Assume a trader owns a large position in a thinly traded stock. If the trader needs to sell the stock soon, he or she may be unable to locate a buyer, or the selling price may be substantially lower than intended, resulting in a financial loss. This is an example of liquidity risk, in which the trader is unable to sell the asset in time to avoid a loss.

A trader may also face liquidity risk if he or she invests in a fund with a lock-up period. The trader cannot redeem their investment during the lock-up period, even if they require cash immediately. This might result in liquidity risk if the trader is forced to sell other assets at a loss in order to pay their financial obligations.

Why it is essential to manage risk?

It cannot be denied that managing risk is one of the most critical aspects of trading. The reason behind this is simple - trading involves a significant amount of uncertainty, and every trade comes with a certain amount of risk. However, by managing risk effectively, traders can protect their capital and minimize losses while increasing their chances of long-term profitability.

The art of managing risk requires discipline, patience, and a thorough understanding of market dynamics. All these factors combined can help traders create a risk management strategy that works best for them. So, if you want to succeed as a trader, make sure to prioritize risk management and make it an integral part of your trading strategy.

Risk Management Strategies

Trading risk management strategies include a collection of tactics and procedures designed to reduce the influence of possible risks on trading operations. Following are some common risk management techniques with examples:

Diversification: Diversification entails spreading trading operations across several markets, instruments, and trading tactics. Traders can limit their exposure to specific risks and boost their prospects of long-term profitability by diversifying. A trader, for example, may take positions in many currency pairings in order to spread their exposure to exchange rate changes.

Let's imagine an investor has a 100,000 rupees portfolio and wants to diversify their holdings to lower overall risk. Stocks, bonds, and real estate investment trusts (REITs) are the three asset classes that the investor decides to divide their portfolio among.

A decision is made to allocate 40% of the portfolio's assets to stocks, 30% to bonds, and 30% to REITs. The investor chooses a number of securities from each asset type to further diversify their holdings. For instance, the investor may choose to invest in businesses from various industries and sectors, such as technology, healthcare, and consumer products, within the allocation of stocks.

The portfolio of the investor may be impacted if the stock market declines, but such losses may be partially offset by increases in the investor's bond or REIT holdings. The investor's losses in a declining real estate market may be partially offset by gains in their stock or bond assets. The investor has lowered their exposure to any one asset class and total risk by diversifying their portfolio.

Position sizing: Position sizing is the process of establishing the optimal size of a trading position depending on the level of risk and the risk tolerance of the trader. Traders can minimise their risk and prevent potential losses by carefully sizing holdings. A trader, may limit the size of their position to a certain proportion of their account balance.

For example, Assume a trader has a 10,000 rupees account balance and wishes to open a long position in a stock trading at 50 rupees per share. The trader decides to utilise a risk management approach that restricts their risk on each one deal to 2% of their account balance. As a result, the trader is willing to lose up to 200 rupees on this trade (10,000 x 0.02).

To determine the proper position size for this trade, divide the maximum amount the trader is willing to risk by the difference between the entry and stop loss prices. Assume the trader places a stop loss at 48 rupees per share. As a result, the difference between the entry and stop loss prices is 2 rupees per share.

To keep the risk at 200 rupees, the trader can only buy 100 shares (200 rupees/2 rupees). This means that the trader has a position of

100 shares, which is worth 5,000 rupees (50 rupees per share x 100 shares).

Hedging: Hedging entails taking counter-positions to decrease exposure to prospective hazards. To decrease their exposure to exchange rate volatility, a trader can take a long position in one currency pair and a short position in another.

Assume a trader has a long position in a stock but is concerned that the stock price will fall in the near future. To protect himself from future losses, the trader chooses to purchase a put option on the stock.

The put option gives the trader the right to sell the stock at a fixed price (the strike price) before the option expires. If the price of the stock falls below the strike price, the trader can exercise the option and sell the stock at the higher strike price, limiting their possible losses.

Assume the trader owns 100 shares of XYZ stock, which is currently trading at 50 rupees per share. The trader purchases a 45 rupees put option with an expiration date of one month from now. The put option costs 3 rupees per share, or rupees 300 in total.

If the stock price falls to 40 rupees per share before the expiration date, the trader can exercise the put option and sell the stock for 45 rupees per share, limiting their possible losses to 5 rupees per share (plus the put option cost). The trader would have lost 10 rupees per share if the put option had not been used.

Risk-reward ratio: calculating the potential reward of a deal in relation to the potential risk. Traders should choose deals with a favourable risk-reward ratio, meaning that the potential benefit outweighs the potential danger. A trader, for example, may aim for a risk-reward ratio of 1:3, which means that the potential reward is three times the potential risk.

For example, Assume a trader wants to buy a stock at 50 rupees with the intention of profiting if the price rises to 55 rupees. The trader places a stop-loss order at 48 rupees, indicating that if the stock falls below this price, they will sell it to reduce their possible losses.

This trade has a potential profit of 5 rupees per share (55 - 50) and a potential loss of 2 rupees per share (50 - 48). As a result, the risk-reward ratio is 2.5 to 1 (5 rupees/2 rupees).

In this case, the trader is ready to risk 2 rupees in order to potentially profit 5 rupees, which indicates that for every dollar risked, they could profit 2.50 rupees. The greater the risk-reward ratio, the more profit a trader may make for every dollar risked.

Risk tolerance & setting risk management goals

Effective risk management in trading involves a number of key components, including risk tolerance and creating risk management objectives.

The degree of risk that a particular trader is willing to accept is referred to as risk tolerance. Understanding one's risk tolerance is crucial before trading because it can guide trading choices and risk management tactics. While traders with a higher risk tolerance might feel more at ease taking on larger positions but may also be willing to accept greater risks, traders with a lower risk tolerance might prefer to take smaller positions and use stop-loss orders to limit losses.

Establishing precise targets and boundaries for managing risks is part of setting risk management goals. This can involve determining acceptable risk-to-reward ratios for transactions, establishing criteria for when to abandon trades, and setting maximum loss limits. Traders can help ensure that their trading activities are in line with their overall risk tolerance and long-term trading goals by creating risk management goals.

Traders can take into account the following aspects when setting risk management objectives:

Risk tolerance: To make sure that their goals and risk preferences are in line, traders should take into account their risk tolerance while defining risk management targets.

Trading goals: Traders should think about their overall trading goals and create risk management targets that support those aims.

Market circumstances: Traders should take the current market conditions into account and modify their risk management objectives as necessary to take these changes into account.

Trading strategy: Traders should think about their trading strategy and create risk management objectives that complement it.

Role of psychology in Trading

In trading, psychology is really important. Successful traders must not only comprehend the markets and trading tactics, but they must also have a strong mental game. Here are some examples of how psychology affects trading:

Emotions: Emotions have the power to greatly influence trading decisions. Overconfidence, greed, and fear can all result in irrational choices and subpar trading results. Traders who are successful must be able to control their emotions and make reasonable, fact-based decisions.

Discipline: Maintaining discipline is essential for profitable trading. Even in difficult market conditions, traders must have the discipline to follow their rules and stick to their trading plan.

Mindset: A trader's thinking can have a big impact on how successful they are. Traders who adopt a growth attitude and see setbacks as chances to grow and learn are better able to withstand market volatility.

Risk Management: Effective risk management is crucial for trading success. The risk factors involved in each deal must be evaluated by traders, who must then manage their exposure accordingly. This necessitates self-control and sound judgement when making decisions.

ॐ

XV
Case Studies

Benefits of case studies

- **Real-world examples:** Case studies can show traders how successful traders have used trading methods and approaches to achieve positive results. This can help traders comprehend how to implement these approaches in their own trading.
- **Analysis of mistakes:** Case studies can also assist traders in analyzing frequent mistakes and hazards made by other traders. Traders can avoid making the same mistakes as others by learning from their mistakes and improving their trading performance.
- **Risk management demonstration:** Case studies can show how successful traders manage risk. Traders can limit possible losses and increase their chances of success by understanding how to handle risk efficiently.
- **Development of trading skills:** Case studies can aid traders in improving their analytical abilities and enhancing their capacity to recognize profitable trading possibilities. Traders can learn how to create their own trading strategy and plan by researching various trading scenarios.

Now here are some real-time trade examples (case studies) given:-

Using Breakout

Case study 1: I selected the latest chart of Oil & Natural Gas for the 1 hour time frame, as shown in *figure 15.1*, and you can clearly see that it is falling since there are more sellers than buyers. This chart has formed a trendline, so all we need to do is wait for it to break that trendline.

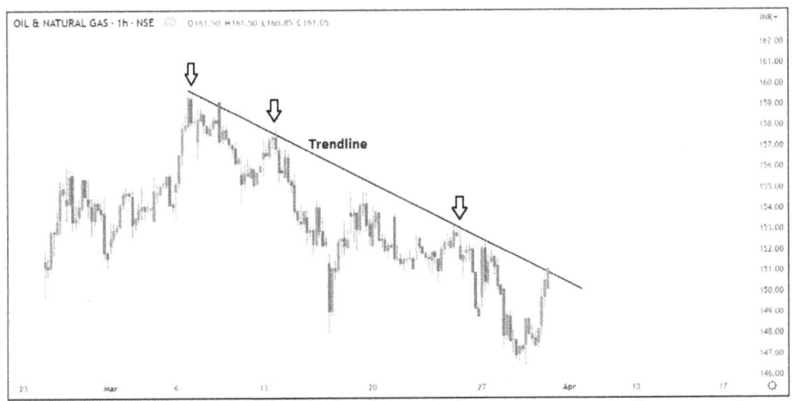

figure 15.1

As you can see in *figure 15.2* on the next page, the market has already broken through the trendline. As soon as it retests the trendline, you should buy at a price of around 151 or 152 rupees as illustrated in figure. Your target is around 160 rupees to the point from which the trend line falls and your stoploss is below the trendline which can only 3 to 4 rupees, here your risk reward ratio is approximately 1 : 2.5

figure 15.2

<u>Case study 2</u>: Here, I've included a Sun Pharmaceuticals chart with a one-day time period that's ideal for swing trading. As you can see in figure 15.3, the price clearly resisted the market three times before finally breaking through the zone at approximately at the price of 130 rupees (approx).

figure 15.3

As it has broken out and retested the zone, it is now safe to enter, so we can buy at 955 rupees (approx), our stoploss is the same as the previous one below the zone at 910 rupees (approx), as shown in the *figure 15.4*, and here we cannot decide the target because there is no pattern here, so we use trailing stoploss and try to cover more profit as the market reacts.

figure 15.4

Using Trend

Case Study 3: In *figure 15.5* on the next page I've provided you the chart of Tata Steel on a one-day time frame. By looking at it, you can quickly determine that it is in an uptrend.

I've simply attached the points of higher highs and lower lows as shown, we must wait for the breakout on the upper side in order to trade the trend.

figure 15.5

Here in *figure 15.6* , market has given breakout and retested the upper trendline.Now is the time to enter the trade. We will enter at around 87 rupees and place our stoploss below the upper trendline at around 82 rupees.We are unable to set a target because there aren't any pattern and we're trading the trend. As a result, we will use a trailing stop loss and try to cover more.

figure 15.6

<u>Case Study 4:</u> In *figure 15.7* I have shown Oil & Natural Gas chart on 4 hours time frame here by seeing it you can analyze that the chart is falling and forming a downtrend.

Joining lower highs we formed a trendline as shown in the figure now wait for the market how it will react it is down trend so will be making the sort position.

figure 15.7

As shown in Figure 15.8 on the next page, during the third rejection of the trendline, we can enter the trade near the trendline as we see a indication of falling.

We can enter at 161 rupees (approx) because it shows a price rejection here and our stoploss is 170 rupees (approx). Because we are trading on the basis of trend of the market and it is not forming any pattern we will be unable to determine the target, so we will use the trailing stoploss.

figure 15.8

Using Support and Resistance

Case Study 5: Figure 15.9 depicts the ITC LTD chart on a 1 day time frame. The price has resisted there four times.

figure 15.9

It indicates that it is a strong support as shown.We can enter trade if it pulls back the price so wait for the confirmation. After taking support on the zone the market gave the indication by forming green candle on the support zone so we can enter at 333 rupees and our stoploss is approx rupees 315 below the support zone. Our target is decide by the risk reward ratio of 1:2 and we can use the trailing stoploss.

figure 15.10

<u>Case Study 6</u>: In *figure 15.11*, I have shown you the Chart of JSW Steel on a higher time frame here we are going to take swing trade.

Simply join all the higher price points of the chart as I joined a resistance will form as shown in the figure. Now wait for the market to take a reversal on the resistance level.

After waiting, we have two opportunities to enter the trade as shown in *figure 15.12* on the next page.

figure 15.11

After seeing the bearish move we can enter the trade at rupees 740 with a stoploss of approximately 800 rupees, and the trendline support level is our target. However, we must use a trailing stoploss because no one knows where the market will go.

figure 15.12

Using Candlestick Patterns

Case Study 7: In *figure 15.13* chart of Axis Bank is shown on 1 day time frame price is consolidating between two levels support and resistance. However, it forms a trendline, and we must now wait for the price to break the trendline. If the price breaks the trendline, we can wait for a retest; however, if you wait, it will be safer for you to trade. As you can see, a bullish engulfing candle appears around support after the trendline is broken.

figure 15.13

We will enter at approximately 640 rupees and set our stoploss at 610 rupees because so many factors are in our favour, such as it breaking the trendline, retesting, and taking support on the support line. Our first goal is the first lower high as shown in *figure 15.14*, and if that is achieved, we will hold the trade up to the second lower high as illustrated in the figure

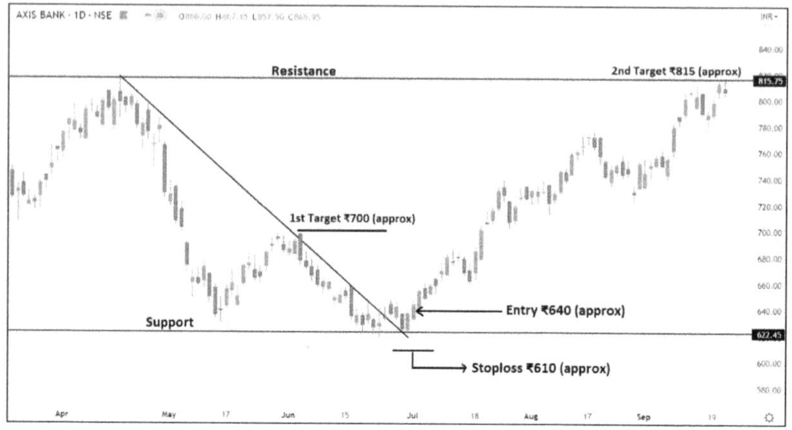

figure 15.14

Case Study 8: In *figure 15.15*, the graph of UPL LTD is presented on a one-day time frame; mark the support level on the higher time frame as I have done; as a result, the indicated level can be used as a support and resistance level in the smaller timeframe.

The resistance level that I utilized here is also displayed in a larger time frame.

As you can see, an inverted hammer, which is a bearish candle, appeared at the resistance level; now, we must wait for the confirmation candle

NOTE: Always use trailing stoploss in each trade because it protects your profits by automatically adjusting the stop loss price as the price of the asset moves in your favor.

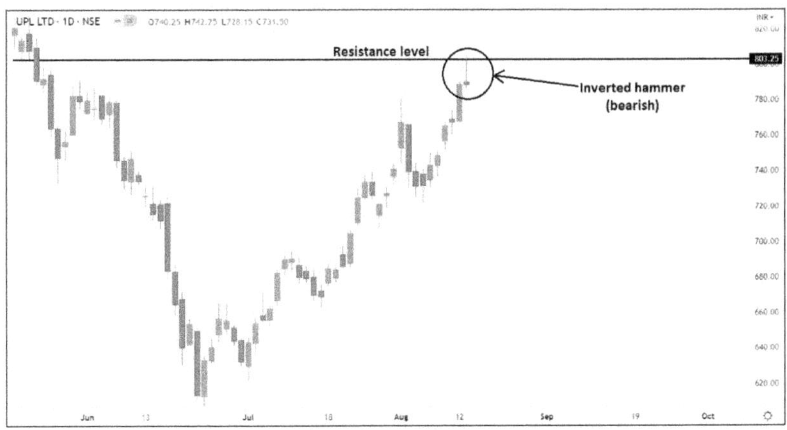

figure 15.15

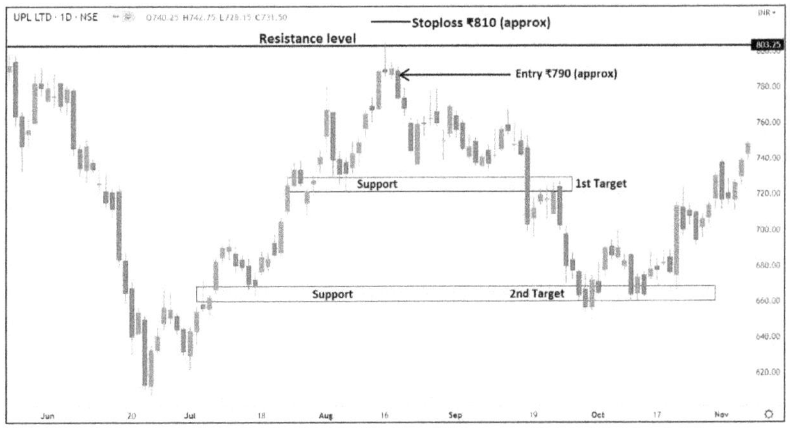

figure 15.16

As you can see in *figure 15.16*, the confirmation candle is formed after the inverted hammer, so we can enter the trade at 790 rupees (approx) and our stoploss is above the resistance level at 810 rupees, and our first target is at the level of higher lows of the previous movement and same for the second target as shown in the figure.

Using Chart Patterns

Case Study 9: In *figure 15.17* chart of MRF LTD is shown on 1 day time frame here you can see symmetrical triangle pattern is formed after waiting price gave breakout and retested at lower trendline of the pattern, we now must patiently wait for the confirmation candle.

figure 15.17

After waiting a big bearish candle formed. It can be seen in *figure 15.18* therefore, we can enter around 88500 rupees (approx) and set our stoploss at 92000 rupees (approx) you can set this according to your capital and risk management.

Our target is defined by higher lows of the pattern, as indicated in the image. These patterns rarely hit our stoploss from my experience 8 trades from the 10 are on our side.

figure 15.18

<u>Case study 10</u>: In *figure 15.19* graph of Hero Motocorp LTD is shown on 1 day time frame so what we haveto do try to find out the support resistance level as I marked the support leveling the figure you can see after marking support , a double top pattern can be seen ,which gave break out.

figure 15.19

Now we know what to do simply wait for the retest or for the closing of the candle below the support zone or for any other confirmation.

After waiting, a bigger bearish candle is formed as you can see in the *figure 15.20* and that is enough to enter in the trade so we can simply enter at 2600 rupees (approx) and our stoploss is at 2720 rupees (approx) and our target is approx 2420 rupees as shown in *figure 15.19*.

figure 15.20

Using Indicators

Case Study 11: Figure 15.21 shows the graph of Bombay dyeing on a one-day time frame with two indicators: moving average exponential and volume. As you can see, the price is in a downtrend and is attempting to change direction by crossing the EMA 50 with increasing volume, as shown in the figure.

figure 15.21

After waiting we see that a green bullish candle crosses the EMA line with good volumes so it is a great opportunity to trade , therefore we enter at 70 rupees and set stoploss at 62 rupees which is below the EMA line. Our target is previous level of support or resistance which I have marked in the *figure 15.22*.

figure 15.22

<u>Case Study 12:</u> In *figure 15.23*, the graph of State Bank of India is shown on 1 day time frame here also same indicators are used as previous example. This graph is in uptrend, we can see the price is consolidating in a zone, after waiting it gave breakout upper side by following the trend now we will wait for candle closing.

figure 15.23

figure 15.24

After waiting we see that a green marubozu candle is formed above the EMA line with good volume as shown in *figure 15.24* so, it can also be a good opportunity to enter so, we will take entry at rupees 545 and our stoploss is 515 and our target near 575 as marked in the figure so here risk reward ratio is 1:1.

NOTE: I believe these examples are sufficient to demonstrate how to trade utilising all of these strategies and tools. After this, spend time with charts and try to find patterns, as well as do paper trading daily on a demo account before making actual trades with your experience you will learn fast.

1. **<u>Develop a trading plan</u>**: A trading plan is necessary to ensure that you trade in a systematic manner. Your strategy should include your entry and exit criteria, risk management strategy, and other essential considerations

2. **<u>Use proper risk management</u>**: When trading price action, risk management is critical. To limit your losses and protect your capital, use stop-loss orders and position sizing

3. **<u>Focus on key price levels</u>**: Pay attention to important price levels such as support and resistance levels, trend lines, and chart patterns. These levels may help in the identification of prospective trading opportunities

4. **<u>Understand market context</u>**: Keep an eye on the market environment and how it affects price action. Price swings can be influenced by news events, economic statistics, and market mood, for example

5. **<u>Keep a trading journal</u>**: Maintaining a trading notebook can assist you in tracking your progress and identifying areas for growth. Keep track of your trades, including entry and exit locations, and compare your results over time

6. **<u>Be patient and disciplined</u>**: Price action trading takes both patience and discipline. Stick to your trading plan and don't rush into trades. Avoid emotional trading and instead concentrate on executing your approach.

☙

<u>Thank you for reading this book and I wish you all the best in your trading endeavors.</u>